UNSTOPPABLE "BY CHOICE"

Jamie Bree

authorHOUSE®

AuthorHouse™
1663 Liberty Drive
Bloomington, IN 47403
www.authorhouse.com
Phone: 833-262-8899

Published by AuthorHouse 08/26/2021

ISBN: 978-1-6655-2926-6 (sc)
ISBN: 978-1-6655-2925-9 (hc)
ISBN: 978-1-6655-2924-2 (e)

Library of Congress Control Number: 2021912009

Print information available on the last page.

The Promise has been given
The Process has been prepared
Persist till you get there
A true story of a young woman's persistance in
following the process to achieve the promise.

Yes, You Can Be Unstoppable and Defy the Odds

But Jesus looked at them and said to them, "With men this is impossible, but with God all things are possible."
Matthew 19:26 New King James Version

CONTENTS

ACKNOWLEDGEMENTS

I wish to first acknowledge my Lord and Savior, Jesus Christ and the precious Holy Spirit who indwells me through whom this work was made possible. Secondly, I give honor to my late Mother and Father who were my best cheerleaders, who never stopped me from pursuing my dreams and aspirations and whom I have heard say in the spirit, you finally finished that book. To my siblings who helped make it easy to accomplish my dreams by helping with my sons, although they never really understood me. I give honor to the men in my life, my three sons, who always believed in me and encouraged me in more ways than they could ever imagine. To the ones who helped me grow in God, my Tabernacle Baptist Church East End family, without whom I could not have grown in my relationship with Christ to where I am today. And to every person who listened, learned and loved me, in spite of me!!

PREFACE/INTRODUCTION

It does not matter how you start, but how you finish. Statistics say you will not make it when life's little U-turns and challenges seem to be winning the battle in your life. And just to be honest, you will only make it to a certain point in this thing called life, without God. Come with me as I tell my story of how God worked it out for my good. You see I thought it was me! I was the smart one, I was the strong one, I was the one making it all happen. I was unstoppable! Little did I know that one day God would reveal to me it was Him alone who was working in my life and I would begin a journey of transformation I never knew possible. Share with me in this journey. You will be encouraged, convicted, motivated and who knows, you may even surrender your will to God!

First, let me say it has taken me mannnnnyyy years to finish this book. Just recently God gave me a message to give His people to "Tell the Story." As I sat meditating on the results of the message, the Holy Spirit said, now it's time for you to "finish" telling your story and write that book. This message was your introduction so let's get going. I thank all those who continued to ask me about the status of my book. I even appreciate those who, without shame, told me about how this one or that one had finished their books and published them while I was still procrastinating. So, I have committed to finish this masterpiece over the next few months, before this pandemic ends. Both my Mother and Daddy and several others mentioned in my book have passed and will not be able to read my book, but I know they all will be proud of me finally completing a dream that began so long ago.

What are the chances of survival for a young female of color from a dysfunctional family, who was under skilled, a high school dropout who left high school at 16 to marry her 17-year-old childhood sweetheart because she was pregnant, had her first son at 17 and had two more sons by age 21? What are the chances of this life becoming remarkable? Yet, this young Black woman who grew up in a low-income neighborhood defied the odds. She would not let adversity or lack stop her. She knew there was more to life than getting married and having children at an early age. She always liked to read and was studious from elementary school through high school. It took extraordinarily little study or homework for her to pass the academic tests. She had a good memory for details. Taking her love for reading from her father, she read everything she came across. She not only went back to high school and graduated, but she achieved academic excellence in all higher education pursuits. She graduated with an Associate's degree in Management from the Community College (cum laude maintaining a 3.5 grade point average), a Bachelor's degree in Business Administration from the university (magna cum laude maintaining a 4.0 grade point average), a Master's degree in Public Administration (cum laude) and from the Bible Seminary and College with a Doctor's in Ministry degree where she maintained a 4.0 grade point average in all her classes. Her search for knowledge was unstoppable and even after receiving a doctor's degree she continued to take classes, attend workshops and conferences to keep her knowledge and skills sharpened.

Her federal government career was marked with countless awards and promotions. She was awarded the highest civil servant award at the mid-point of her federal career. Her achievements were continual as where her promotions from the lowest general schedule grade to the highest. She retired at the age of 52 after 30 years of federal government service. She started another career one year after retiring and continues in that profession at the writing of this story. She continues to have an impact on her family and community. Her motto is "If I can help somebody while traveling along this way, my living not be in vain."

Her Type A personality and *"Make it Happen"* philosophy of life were the tools she believed helped her to accomplish these things. She has since learned that nothing in her life could have manifested itself had it not been for Jesus Christ. Her relationship with Jesus as Lord of her life is the most exciting experience she could ever have chosen. Although her BC (Before she surrendered to Christ) attitude and behavior caused her to believe that her know how, tenacity, dedication, commitment, knowledge, and "difference" helped her to pull herself up by her 'boat straps'. But, God! One day God spoke to her heart and said "Little girl, I knew you before you were placed in your mother's womb, I gifted you, equipped you, protected you, provided for you and saved you so that this would be your life." From that day forward she realized the hand of God on her life and accepted God as her personal Savior, developing a growing an intimate relationship with Him as her Lord and Savior. Now she knows it was not her that accomplished all these things, but she gives God all the glory for the great things he has done in her life. She realizes none of her many achievements come close to the relationship she has with Christ.

Her story may be like many others today, but she believes there is someone out there in this great universe that will benefit from the life she has lived. She has made some decisions that have affected her both positively and negatively, but she presses on for the prize of the high calling in Jesus Christ.

Many have attested to her fortitude and willingness to share her story in hopes that it will encourage you to be "Unstoppable," while achieving great things against the odds, if you make the choice to do so.

This is her story.

THE JOURNEY BEGINS

It was one of those dreary days in the community. The sun had not completely gone down over the World War ll housing project that we called home. When I think back on my early years, my mind is flooded with lots of memories. We were one of the many families fortunate enough to have both parents in the home. During those days most homes had both the mom and dad in the home. The average family size was about five children. We played in our neighborhood, came in the house or at least in the yard when the corner light went on and everyone looked out for each other. Our community exemplified the phrase "it takes a village" to raise a child. Any adult felt comfortable praising or correcting all the children in the neighborhood. They would even load their cars with kids needing rides to school events or going to the local skating rink or bowling alley. Even though the neighbors would help with transportation, the majority of our transportation was by foot. Yes, we walked almost everywhere we went. I remember we had a station wagon that Mama would drive on Sunday to take all of us and some neighborhood kids to our neighborhood church. We lived in a mostly segregated neighborhood, although a couple of white families moved in a few years later. There were more white families in the housing complex that was a few blocks from ours. These were the only white people, other than the Jewish brothers who owned the local grocery store, and Mama's domestic work employer that we had contact with.

There were no Big I's and Little U's in our neighborhood. We were all similarly situated. We were all families of Shipyard workers who did life together in a closely knit Black community. Most of the families dealt with the same struggles in life. As children we were taught to respect the elderly and to obey our parents. Our house was near the front of the housing complex which was close to the Elementary school and shopping area. Our Elementary School was only a hop and skip across the ditch from where we lived. The strip mall, as it would be called today, had the Jewish family run grocery store, a barber shop, pool hall and restaurant/bar. They were conveniently located from our house on the other side of the field making quick trips to the store effortless.

We could sleep with our doors open at night with no thoughts that anyone would try to break in. We did not have air conditioning in our two-bedroom house, so it was always nice to sleep in front of the door and feel the air flowing in. We used a floor fan and had window fans to cool the house.

Most of the Mothers in the neighborhood were homemakers and some, like my Mom, did domestic work for white families. My Mother had what I call, two sets of children. My three sisters and I migrated with my Mother from North Carolina when we were about four, three, two, and my little sister was less than one year old. Because my father had gotten a job at the Shipyard, he brought us to Virginia to live. We were in Virginia about two years before the second set of four children were born.

THE FAMILY

I am blessed, unlike so many, to have a large family of seven siblings and an extended sister who grew up with us from her teenage years. Being the second oldest of the four girls in the first set, just made me that sister. Many have said that I was different from my other sisters. My Mother used to tell me I was just like my Daddy. She meant it sometimes in a negative way, seeing a character trait in me that she disliked in him. I enjoyed being compared to my Daddy because he was very special to me and he was smart. I remember when he would sit us down on the floor and read the Bible and we would play games and he would give us candy if we answered the questions correctly. Although we had some not so good times because of his drinking, I really loved my Daddy. We celebrated the same birthdate for years and I enjoyed saying I was born on my Daddy's birthday. I would say that my Mom held onto me until after midnight so that I would be born on his birthday. This went on for years, until the inevitable happened!! We were preparing to go on a cruise one year and I had to get my Daddy a passport. He needed his original birth certificate, so we sent the appropriate request to the North Carolina Office of Vital Statistics. Was I surprised to learn his actual birthday was six days later than the day he had celebrated, along with me! That was so devastating to me. All these years, about

40 some years, I had celebrated my birthday with my Daddy only to find out he was born on a different day. I remember telling him how I was disappointed we didn't have the same birthday and he said jokingly, well change your date to mine!

I was the second child in the family. My oldest sister was the favored one. My Mother was an only child and my sister was the first granddaughter of my maternal Grand Mother. There was nothing that she would ask for that she did not get. Oh, it seems so familiar now, my sister and I shopping with my Grand Mother at the local big department store downtown in this little southern North Carolina town. Whenever my sister asked my Grand Mother for anything, it seemed without much delay to appear instantly. I often felt my requests were frequently delayed. Sometimes it would show up later or later never came for whatever reasons. Well! such is life was my attitude. My oldest sister frequently went with my Grand Mother to a lot of places while I was left to look after my other two sisters. We went to my Grand Mother's house in North Carolina almost every summer from adolescence to our teenage years. I enjoyed our summers in the south especially as we got older and we were able to get jobs. I loved being able to work and make money although my sisters complained about how early we had to get up. We were picked up every morning in an open back pickup truck. We worked in the tobacco field and made very little money, but I was just happy to be making my own money. We started out as tobacco handers making $5 a day, the loopers made $7 a day and the primers made $25 a day. Most of the younger children were handers just handing a fist full of tobacco making sure the stalks all pointed the same way, to the older women who were loopers. But only the men could serve as primers. I wanted to be a looper so I learned how to loop the tobacco on the stick that would be hung in the barn to dry and got my $7 a day. I wanted to prime, or cut the tobacco, but my gender didn't allow me to. One year after we went back home from summer break, my oldest sister did not come back to Virginia with us. She wanted to stay with my Grand Mother and my Mom let her stay for an entire year. She went to school in North Carolina.

Music was a central focus in our household. Both my Mom and Dad liked music and music was always playing. We had a piano in the living room of our two-bedroom house. I do not know where it came from, but I was always trying to play it. I never had piano lessons, but I loved teaching myself the few tunes I knew. In my music class at school, I learned the notes and I would get a music book and teach myself a few notes. I put these notes together into a few tunes and started playing some tunes, a classic *Green Onions* and another song I can't remember now. My Daddy would have his friends at the house and he would ask me to play them a song. When I did, they would always give me a quarter for playing the piano. I was making a few coins with this newly acquired skill. As I reflect on those times, I do not know if they gave me the money because it sounded good or if it was just because a little girl was playing the piano to entertain them. Either way, it became a "hustle" for me.

My love for music and my ability to dance quite well, got me and my two sisters a place on a dance team when we were about 14 and 15 years old. There were seven in the group, five girls and two guys. We were under-aged teenagers being exploited by a man who had us making our rounds in local clubs showing off our dancing skills. One of the guys was the primary choreographer, but we all contributed our moves and worked well together and had lots of fun. We were good too! Our "agent" got us gigs on the same stage with some noted artists in those days, such as Isaac Hayes and Ike and Tina Turner. After each dance, we went to the local burger place or hot dog stand where we would each get paid with a burger or hot dog of our choice. I do not remember ever getting paid money. Because we all loved to dance, I doubt if we were upset about getting paid in food! But I know our "agent" got paid dollars.

My Mom always sang with the church choir. She started a children's choir at church and introduced drums to our traditional Baptist Church. She said the church needed to grow with the times. If they wanted to keep these kids in church, they would have to do something to maintain their interest and music was it. She loved music and began a choir in a women's religious organization of which she was a member. That choir traveled throughout the area performing at churches in Tidewater and even in some other states. She also started a choir made up of people from local churches in the area. I sang with the choir along with about six other women and three men. Mama also started a community choir of about twenty young people between the ages of six to 26 years old. They were a special group of young people and God's anointing was all over them. The choir director had a great voice, was a disciplinarian and very strict about the choir singing their parts and being in tune. He did not allow the choir members to just sing anything. He required them to sing to the glory of God and rehearsals would sometimes last for several hours until they had the song just the way he wanted it. This community choir opened for many great Gospel groups who visited the Coliseum such as Slim and the Supreme Angels and James Cleveland. They sang at churches throughout Virgina and I was honored to serve as their manager. My Mom and another friend designed all their uniforms and they always looked professional. We had bookings in North Carolina, Maryland and Georgia and had a reputation for being one of the best Gospel groups in the area.

My Mom worked as a housekeeper when she was not working with the choirs. The family she worked for was white and lived in the upper section of our town, about ten miles away from our World War II housing community. Mama would take the bus to their house and walk the three miles from the main street to their house which sat at the back of their community. She was a nice lady and she had one daughter who was about our age. She willingly shared the clothes her daughter had out grown with Mama who would always bring them home for us to share.

I remember one year when I was about 13 or 14, Mama took me to work with her. I wanted a leather coat, so she let me help her perform domestic work to raise the money for my coat. And I did! That summer I was able to save the money I made to buy my first knee length leather coat that Fall! I remember it was black and so soft. It cost a whopping $25 brand new! I was so proud of my accomplishment. Because there were so many of us in the family, Mama welcomed that fact that I wanted to work and buy my own coat. I cannot remember her reaction, but I am sure she was thankful for my initiative and ability to save and buy myself a coat.

DOING THE POSSIBLE

Being responsible and working kinda shaped my life and helped me to learn that nothing was impossible if you were willing to work for it. I learned my priorities would have to change and I would have to be willing to make sacrifices for the things I wanted. I saw making an income as a means to an end, and I will never forget the thrill I experienced from earning my own money to buy what I wanted. These lessons were the foundation for many of my life's decisions.

One of these foundations was responsibility. The school was just across the field from our house, so we walked. Our schools were primarily segregated, and we had a couple Latin teachers in our High School, a few white teachers, and a few black men. But, the majority of our teachers were black women. Our Elementary school teachers knew our parents and would not hesitate to correct our behavior when it was needed. In those days, the teachers knew the parents of all their students and knew your brothers and sisters. Because there were four of us sisters in the school at the same time, the teachers knew we were related and expected us to act a certain way. They would often compare our behaviors to each other and likewise expect the younger ones to behave like the older siblings. Because we were in walking distance from our Elementary school, most of the time we went home for lunch. Many times our friends would come home with us for lunch and my mama would have something prepared for all of us. When she started working, we took our lunch to school and were not allowed to come home during the day if she was not home. Although my parents did not attend parent teacher meetings, they were well aware of what we were doing in school. They knew our teachers and the teacher would call the parents to keep them informed of things that were happening.

I always enjoyed school and loved to read, just like my Daddy. The kids I hung around with liked to read as well. Under today's standards we would have been called "nerds." Most of my friends' Moms were teachers at the schools we attended. I was involved in other clubs and activities in Junior High and High school, but my focus was mostly on academics. Academics were very important to me. I loved making good grades and would get upset when my grades fell below an A. My extra-curricular activities included being part of the photography club, the band, pep squad, and in High School, I was a cheerleader. One of my best friends was also on the cheering squad. Although we were good friends, our families parenting skills were different.

Family life was what it was and I soon came to understand that we did not have a lot of the things other families had. My Mother did what she could to make sure we had everything we needed. We knew we were loved, but we didn't get many hugs or hear the words "I love you." Mom did not allow us to argue among ourselves and would constantly remind us, that's your sister, that's your brother, you don't fight each other but you have to look out for each other. One year my maternal Grand-Mother became ill and came to live with us. Although our two-bedroom home was small and included seven children, my niece who was my oldest sister's child and, my

Mom and my Dad, we were able to make space for her. We put her hospital bed in the middle of the living room. Eventually as the older girls started getting married and leaving home at a young age, my Grand-Mother's bed was placed in our bedroom. We had a pull-out couch in the living room which became a sleeping space for three of my younger siblings and later a sleeping place for me, my son and my husband when he was home on leave.

During the time my Grand-Mother lived with us, I became pregnant and got married. A year later she died. She provided quite a bit to our family. She was financially well-off and helped my Mom pay the rent and buy food and other things we needed. I don't think she liked my Daddy very much. She used to cook the food and then put it away to keep him from eating. She would also remind him he spent his money drinking so he wasn't getting any of our food. I remember hearing conversations that she had picked out this other man, who was light-skinned and from a family with money for my Mama to marry. She did marry this man but they didn't stay together long. My Mother was her only child and she wanted the best for her. My Dad worked in the local Coca-Cola plant in their small North Carolina hometown and lived across town from my Grand-Mother and Mom. My Grand-Mother was part Native American. Her Mother was a full-blooded Native American and her father was a black man. During our summer visits to North Carolina, we went to my Grand-mother's house. She owned her own home and we were told my Grand-father had been a business owner. I never met my Grand-father.

One year my Mom's aunt came to visit us in Virginia and she told us some stories about our Grand-father. She said he was the first black man in town to own a car and that he bought another car for his business foreman to drive. When my Mother was young and would go into the big department store downtown, my Grand-father would tell the store clerks to give her whatever she wanted. I never met either of my Grand-fathers either paternal or maternal. I didn't know very much about either one of them only what I heard from some of the stories that were told.

My father's side of the family included about 14 children. I remember meeting many of my aunts and uncles growing up. Many of them drank alcohol and died at an early age. I remember one of my aunt's lived in New York and she and her husband were financially well off. I remember many times they came to visit us driving a big Cadillac and bringing us great gifts. My father lived the longest of his brothers and sisters. He and his youngest sister in North Carolina were very close. We became close to our first cousins in North Carolina. My oldest cousin was the first grand-son in the family and my sister was the first grand-girl. We still maintain contact with my cousins who still live in North Carolina. Although I don't know much about my paternal Grand-father, I do remember my paternal Grand-mother. She loved to cook and whenever we came for visits, we would look forward to enjoying her molasses bread or pudding, as she called it. She was a kind lady who didn't seem to take much junk off anyone. After giving birth to 14 children, it's no guess she didn't take much mess! She was kind to us but insisted that we stay in a kids place and not get into grownups business.

I have very fond memories of my father. My father loved chocolate candy and was very particular about his "Hersey's kisses." He kept them in the refrigerator and told us not to bother his candy. That's why it was always a treat when we got a piece of candy - we saw it, but could not touch it. My father worked in the local Shipyard and always went to work. Later when I was around middle school age, I remember him doing a lot of excessive drinking, but it did not stop him from going to work. Regardless of how drunk he may have been the night before, it did not stop him from walking walk across that bridge from the housing community and going to the Shipyard. He was responsible about going to work, but not very responsible about handling his money. For a long time when he got paid on Friday, he would get drunk and more times than not, get mugged and have his money taken from him before he got home. Of course, we had financial issues as a result. The Sherriff would leave a warrant on our door for the rent on many occasions, although we were never actually evicted. My Mama would always make sure the money came in from somewhere to pay the rent. We would, however, have our lights turned off, so it was nothing to be sitting in the dark eating or reading by candle light.

We didn't have a television at the time so we listened to a lot of radio. I believe that's where our love for music came from. When we got a TV it was a rental we had to put 25 cents in the slot to turn it on. We had limited television watching as a result. However, we got more TV time when one of my smart sisters, not sure which one, figured out how to jimmy the slot with a clothes hanger giving us more time without having to pay the 25 cents.

Life was very simple and we played outside with our friends under the street lights and in the yard of our neighbors across the street where there was a big oak tree. We knew when the street lights came on to be in the yard. My Mom did not have to call our names to remind us to come in. We knew we would get into big trouble and not be able to play outside for a while. She didn't say we were "punished" she just said you will keep your behinds in the house until I tell you to go outside again. While we were in the house, we cleaned and learned how to cook. The meals my Mom made were simple, so I caught on pretty quickly. But I enjoyed baking. She taught me to bake cakes from scratch and I helped her during the holidays make the family cakes. My Dad always wanted chocolate so we always made a chocolate cake for any event. Chocolate also became my favorite cake. We had a big Christmas meal but did not get a lot of toys or clothes. Instead of a lot of Christmas gifts, we got a cardboard box with raisins, apples, oranges, nuts and a few pieces of Christmas candy. We were thankful to get that! If we got any toys, it was only one special toy or one new outfit of clothing. It was okay with us just to get our box of candy, nuts and fruit.

MARRIAGE AND MOTHERHOOD

A young man appeared on our door step one day to visit my older sister when I was frantically making my way to the store to get our dinner for the day - hotdogs and beans. He almost got knocked over as I went flying out the door. I did not remember him at first, but he and my sister had attended Elementary school together. He had moved out of town to live with his Grand-mother and was now returning to Virginia to live with his Mother, Father, his older brother and sister. Although my sister was not at home, he decided to wait until I came back from the store so we could talk. He was such a nice-looking guy who was dressed in a grey shark skin suit, something you did not see young men wearing unless they were going to church. He had a great smile and nice eyes. He was friendly to my Mom and she invited him in to wait in the kitchen where she was. She knew his Mom and Dad because we all grew up in the same area. So, she was engaged in a conversation with him about his parents as I continued my journey to the grocery store.

Later I remembered his older sister being friends with my sister and actually being the one who helped me understand my menstrual cycle. You would think with four girls, Mom would have talked to us about those things. Maybe because she was a spoiled only child, her Mom readily took care of those things for her. I believe she and her Dad had a better relationship so maybe her Mom did not take the time to educate her on changes she could expect her body to go through. My Mom had her first live birth at age 19 and she continued to have a child almost every year thereafter. Sisters, please make sure your younger girl friends and sisters understand their bodies.

We learned about our bodies from the older girls. I remember coming on my period and thinking I had done something wrong. I loved climbing trees and thought I must have slipped and injured myself when I saw the blood in my pants. I went in and asked my sister and she said she would ask her friend. Later when Mama came home, I told her what had happened, and she told me to get a rag and put it in my panties and wash it out every time I had to change it. We did not have sanitary pads, at least we could not afford them during these earlier times. I remember thinking how nasty this was, washing blood out of rags, letting them dry and using them again, but that is what we did. My Mama did tell me that I could now get pregnant so watch out for those little boys. This conversation just went in one ear and out the other because I had no idea how to get pregnant nor was I even thinking about such things. My sister's older friends had those talks with us and said you can get pregnant when you have sex with a boy. I immediately thought, oh no, that will not happen to me.

This young man who stopped by our house later became my boyfriend. He was a lot of fun and kept me laughing all the time. We took long walks and on occasion, rode the city bus to the beach. He was a gentleman and would always walk on the outside of the sidewalk. He said if a car came it would have to hit him before it could hit me. I felt protected! One night in June we were outside on the back steps kissing and he asked me if he could "touch" it. I had no idea what he was going to touch or with what. I was so naïve! I was a virgin, so I did not know what "touch it" really meant. At any rate, a few months later, I did not have a period and after consulting with an older friend I discovered I was pregnant. I had started having my period at the age of 15. Since I'd only been having my period a few months, I did not know what was going on. When I told my Mom, she took me to the family doctor who confirmed my suspicion. When I told my boyfriend I was pregnant, he was happy. He joined the Army and when he returned home from Basic Training in December, he came to talk to my Mama about marrying me.

My Mom insisted that I get married and was in total agreement with my boyfriend. It did not seem of any importance that I did not love him or even know what love entailed. Marriage was something special and I had not planned to get married or have children until I finished school and got a job. My Mom agreed that he could marry me although he did not ask my dad. He told her that his career in the Army would allow him to take care of me and the baby. He said he loved me. Even though little naïve me had no understanding of love. Mom said it was better for me to marry someone who loved me and assured me that I would learn to love him. So, at seven months pregnant, I stood in my parent's living room before the kerosene/wood burning stove and married my childhood sweetheart who had wooed me.

My ceremony was as simple as they come. There was no great fanfare, no fancy wedding dress, brides' maids, groomsmen, flower girls, ring bearers, none of that. I wore a simple light blue two-piece suit made from some crinkly fabric. My Dad never really seemed happy about my getting married. In fact, he actually sat on the front steps during the ceremony and did not come into the house. My

Mom's Pastor was the officiant. We had not had any kind of pre-martial counseling. Not many people attended the wedding.

My Mom's best friend, and I believe my oldest sister and two younger sisters, attended. My Mom's friend was an extremely big woman who looked white. She would always drive my Mom places she needed to go. Her husband was a little man who seemed to always yield to her every desire. She gave me a job ironing her bras and bed sheets and paid me a little money when I was about 13 years old. Her bras were so large they covered the entire ironing board. She had adopted a little girl and I was her babysitter. She lived about four blocks from us which was only a few minutes' walk from our house. I would go there at least two times a week to iron for her and babysit her daughter.

After the marriage ceremony, Mom's friend took us riding through the neighborhood blowing the car horn which was a tradition at the time. We drove to the Italian restaurant where my older sister worked and the owner gave us a bottle of Italian red wine. After that we returned to my parent's home. Later that night, we celebrated our nuptials by going to the movie theater to see what, I cannot remember. Going to the movies became one of our favorite things to do. I remember thinking about what had taken place in my life and had all kinds of anxiety about what I would be facing. I had no idea what was going to be required of me as a wife and Mother. The only example I had was my Mom and she and my Dad didn't always get along because of his drinking. There was a lot of arguing and mental abuse in our house and this was the foundation for my preparation as a wife and Mother. My Mom was a good Mom and did everything she could for us kids. We were never hungry or homeless and although we didn't have much, we were envied by a lot of other families because of our closeness. So equipped with what I had seen my Mom do, I was prepared to settle into a life that I had not been properly prepared for, but God!

I did not return to school after the Christmas holiday break my eleventh year of school because of my pregnancy. I was married that January and was still trying to understand what was next. I did not want to stop school, but during those days you were not looked at too favorably as a young pregnant girl in school, even though I was married. I was a naïve 16-year-old girl who did not even know how she got pregnant. I had not written pregnancy and marriage into my immediate future. I was only a junior in high school and had goals to finish school, go on to college, get a good job and have my own place. That plan got changed along the way. It was delayed but not forgotten. There is a saying that goes "delayed but not denied." I can attest to that!

My life at my parent's house was not much fun after I got married. My father and I, whom I had had a close relationship with during my earlier years, began having more and more problems. He seemed to be drinking more and always angry. I remember one day he told me to do something and I didn't respond as quickly as he thought I should and he threw a footstool at me yelling, "I know you heard me while you sitting there with your pregnant self." I will never forget that day. The footstool did not hit me, but I remember the sound of disappointment in his voice. My Dad had never really disciplined us. The only time he executed any punishment was when we were disciplined for going into the kitchen with our pajamas on. He hit the four of us with a newspaper while we kneeled at our beds. My Mom was the disciplinarian. I felt so bad that I had been a disappointment to him and at this point I knew I needed to move out of their house and get my own place. I had given my boyfriend an ultimatum when he asked me to marry him and that was that he would get me my own place. My place didn't come quickly, but eventually we did move down the street from my parents into one of the WWII houses.

I was now going to the Army clinic for my doctor's appointments during my pregnancy. One March morning Mama and her friend took me to the Army post for my monthly check-up. When the doctor at the clinic examined me, he sent me directly to the hospital and called ahead to tell them to admit me because I was about to give birth. Upon arrival at the hospital, the orderly told me to take a seat in a wheelchair while he checked me in. By now my pains were getting more intense, but I obeyed anyway. The young soldier at the desk asked me why I was there. I naïvely told him the doctor said I was going to have a baby. The desk clerk asked me if I was sure I was about to deliver a baby since I did not look like I was nine months pregnant. About that time the phone rang, and the doctor asked if had I arrived, the young man said, yes, but he was not sure what to do with me. The doctor ordered him to get me to delivery right then!! A scurrying of activity ensued, and I was wheeled up to the delivery room and began being prepped to deliver my baby. They shaved my vagina, which was strange to me since I already did not have much hair there. Then they rolled me into a room with other women who were in labor. My labor pains were not very excruciating, so I could not understand why so many of the women were screaming and yelling. I remember getting out of my bed and trying to comfort other women and was yelled at to get back in the bed before I dropped my baby on the floor. I was trying to be helpful especially since no one was there with me as I was preparing to bring my baby into the world.

My baby boy came weighing in at 5 pounds and 10 ounces and was 20 inches long. He had a lot of hair on his head. I did not know what I was going to name him, and Mama's friend suggested we name him after his father since he was the first boy. So being obedient, that is what I did. I remained in the hospital a few days then went home. I went back to my Mom and Dad's house with my little baby boy. That pull-out couch in the living room became our bed and life started to happen. A few months later when my spouse came home on leave, I got pregnant with my second son. He was being assigned to North Carolina and my older son and I went with him.

BECOMING A YOUNG ADULT

This was the first time I had lived away from my family. We started married life with a child with no idea what we were doing. We were young, inexperienced, and were faced with many bumps and challenges in the marriage. The first place we lived was in a home with another family. We had the room downstairs and it was okay for our little family. The landlady was nice, but we knew once our second baby came, the place would not be big enough for two children, so we were always looking for a larger place.

We found a place that was on the other side of town from where we were living. We rented a small apartment that was part of a big home owned by a "well to do" black woman. She was genuinely nice to us and went out of her way to make sure we were comfortable in our space. We were introduced to a style of living to which we were not accustomed. The back apartment was fully equipped with a small bedroom, kitchen, bathroom and living room. We had the baby crib in the front room and the house had a nice pond in the back yard that had lots of goldfish. This became my place of escape. When my Mom came to visit, we would sit out in the back and watch the goldfish swim in the pond. I remember fantasizing that one day I would have a nice place like this with water in the back yard. Our landlady entertained a lot and was a great cook. She allowed us to have the leftovers from her parties and they were always good. I remember one time she had these little chickens left over and she asked if we wanted them. I had never seen anything like them before and after tasting them, I found them to be really tasty. Later I discovered they were called Cornish hens!

During that year that we lived in North Carolina, our marriage took many turns. Coupled with the fact we were so young and we didn't have any kind of premarital counseling and truthfully, we didn't have great marriage role models, we didn't know how to handle the issues that started to present themselves in our marriage. Our marital problems became intense and I was not prepared to deal with the upheavals caused by my husband's alcohol use and frequent separations. I was often concerned during these times of separations that something bad may have happened. I would constantly call the hospitals to see if he had been brought in due to an accident. His reasons for these absences were acceptable because we did not have a car and had to depend on others to get around.

Although I had friends who took me to the grocery store, most of the time I would walk. I enjoyed walking to the USO which was not far from the house to roller skate. That was my outlet and it helped me to deal with life. My oldest son cried a lot and I didn't know what to do. He was fed, dry and comfortable. I just didn't know how to stop him from crying, so many times I would leave him in his crib and go skate for about an hour. Never thinking about child endangerment!! God kept me and my son from danger during those times when I left him alone. I did not hold him a lot because I had been taught this spoiled a child. Little did I know just holding him would make him feel better and cause him to stop crying as much. These memories are the reason I praise God now. My heart is filled with thanksgiving that he did not allow anything bad to happen to us and always provided the protection we needed.

The day my second son was born his father was at work and my neighbor called him to come home quickly telling him I was in labor. He and my neighbor were so excited about my being in labor that when she got there to transport me to the hospital to give birth, she left me standing on the porch. When they realized the error of their ways, the car stopped suddenly and pulled back onto the driveway as he jumped out to help me into the car. We went to the Army hospital and it was not long after we arrived that I gave birth to my second son who weighed in at 5 pounds 11 and one half ounces. He was born one year and 10 days later than my first son and weighed one ounce more.

He was such a good baby. He very seldom cried and played by himself with, what I called, the angels, most of the day while lying in his crib smiling and cooing. As I think back on it, my first son probably felt my stress and tension about not knowing how to handle him and not really being aware of what was going on in my life. By the time, my number two son arrived, I was less stressed and a little more confident. Even though we had money issues, life was a little better.

Our marital problems continued but I learned to deal with them. Many times I would threaten to leave and take the boys with me. He would then become all mushy and apologetic declaring that his behavior would change. He had started hanging out with the guy who lived in the same house where we lived. His wife and I became good friends and we were company for each other. When our kids were born, they shared the same name. After her baby was born, she moved back home. I later found out they were not married.

I had married friends who would help me understand this union called marriage and give me a hand in caring for my babies. I got together frequently with some of the older ladies who did not work outside the home. Each day we visited each other and talked about what was required in a marriage. They adopted me as their little sister saying they had to look out for me because I was the youngest in the group and had two babies already at such a young age. I am sure we had some great conversations about being married and all, but I cannot remember much other than cooking, playing cards and watching the daily soap operas or "stories" as we called the daily dramas. Each day we got together I always made sure I would leave in enough time to go home and prepare dinner for my family. My friends said having dinner ready for my family was a mark of being a good wife. I also remember my Mama telling me that I had to make sure my family was fed before I did anything else. After being in North Carolina about two years, my husband got orders to go overseas and my two sons and I returned to Virginia to begin life without him.

LIFE'S TWISTS AND TURNS

Pregnancy and marriage were not part of the plan for my future. I returned home and my family helped me with the boys allowing me to return to finish high school. We moved into our very own two-bedroom WWII duplex apartment down the street from my parents and other siblings. It was nice having my own place. Later my sister, who was a year younger than I, and her daughter, who was the same age as my oldest son, moved in with us. My two sons, my sister, and her daughter and I, began life together. I was back in school and only had one year and a half to finish all my credits. I dedicated myself to finishing and graduated a year later than I would have graduated had I not dropped out. I was really happy with my achievements and really thankful to my family for helping look after the boys while I was finishing school.

During this separation, we wrote each other regularly. Then all of a sudden, the mail stopped coming. I continued to write but did not get any letters back for long periods of time. I was back in school and studying but something was missing. I didn't have any friends outside of my family and I missed having friends to go to the movies and enjoy an occasional meal. I reconnected with an old friend from the 8th grade. I am not sure where or when but we started meeting and talking. I had been a cheerleader and he was on the basketball team. He had graduated a few years earlier and was in the Shipyard Apprentice School. He became more appealing since I had no other relationships. We started dating, having dinner and enjoying an occasional movie. He was very nice and we enjoyed each other's company. Life took a different turn and the inevitable happened. My marital relationship became even more strained. My friend got married and I was left along again.

My spouse returned from his overseas assignment and we remained married although our marriage had taken another devastating turn. I lived a life where forgiveness had been expressed but not really experienced. In retrospect, I was overcome with guilt and shame which caused things in my marriage to get even worse.

It was at this point that my independence kicked into high gear. One day I asked for 15 cents to put with my dime to buy myself a soda and he told me I did not need a soda. I was infuriated and made a vow at that very moment that he would never decide what I needed or did not need again. I was going to get a job. Since he had gotten out of the Army, he was also looking for a job. He tried lots of things, but never found anything that really satisfied him. He worked at an auto repair shop but after coming home with dirty hands, decided this was not for him. He drove the bread truck and delivered bread to the local stores. This did not satisfy either. Then he drove the City bus. Eventually he re-enlisted in the Army. We agreed to remain married but somewhere deep within my heart, I knew that we would not make it. Call it self-fulfilling prophesy or whatever, but it was not working. I continued to believe all the unpleasant behavior was because of my infidelity. Maybe I never really did forgive myself, even though he said he had forgiven me. My focus now was on getting a job. There was a plan taking shape that I was not unaware of.

I had dropped out of typing class in high school because I had no desire to be a typist for anyone, nor did I think I would ever need this skill. However, when I decided to pursue full-time employment, the program that was available through the local community economic opportunity office and a local federal agency required me to be able to type at least 25 words per minute. There was just this little problem, I could not type. But I was determined to get a job. The Civil Rights Act had been passed in 1964 and many government agencies were working on programs to integrate their workplaces. The government agency had decided to institute this clerical training program to bring minorities into predominately white clerical positions at the federal agency. I borrowed a manual typewriter, covered the keys on the typewriter, got a typing book from the local library, and taught myself to type. When I took the typing test, I had the required 25 words per minute with 47 errors! Thank God they did not subtract for errors. I was now eligible to apply but there were no spaces available in the first class which had begun in February 1969.

Three months later, I got a call that a trainee had dropped out and there was a vacancy, but I would have to play catch up if I wanted to attend the class already in session. I was ready to go to work, so I said, yes, I could do it. So that May, at the age of 20 I began my assignment as a clerical trainee. The Director encouraged the agency to let me start even though the class had already been in session for three months ensuring them that she felt comfortable I could handle it. I had met with the Director during the application process and she said she saw a lot of potential in me and believed if I put my mind to it, I could do it. I just wanted a job and if typing was involved, so be it.

Because of her recommendation, I was accepted into the program and was determined to work hard to catch up on the three months of assignments that I had missed. Because my typing skills were low, I spent most of my time outside of the classroom teaching myself to type. The other classes were not a problem for me even though I had never done shorthand or knew what office procedures entailed, I was a fast learner. The classes were typing, English, math, shorthand, and effective office procedures. After six months in the classroom, we were assigned to job sites on the Center as clerical assistants. We were "under-privileged and under-skilled" and this program was intended to ultimately help us get clerical jobs with the federal government. At the end of the program we were given the Federal Civil Service Entrance Exam. We needed to get at least a score of 70 to be qualified to be placed on the list to become permanent federal government employees.

The program included intensive classroom instruction and job placement at select sites. This was my first time working in an office and I really enjoyed it. We spent one month on each site and had job descriptions and supervisors who would evaluate our performance and character. I worked on three job sites. We were evaluated after each assignment. My evaluations included such accolades as cooperative, ambitious, self-confident, neat in appearance, congenial, business like, industrious, etc. I enjoyed organizing the office, performing the administrative duties, but I was not too happy with typing. I still made a lot of errors and used a lot of correction tape and typing erasers whenever I had a typing project to complete.

There were two primary teachers who were extremely helpful and concerned about our success. They both have passed, but they made some great strides in their lives towards helping others achieve. They were the Chief of the Typing Section for the Center and her Assistant who were both white women. We also had a math teacher who was a quiet spirited and very smart African American woman. She looked white and was one of the few Black Mathematicians at the Center. She would later be recognized in a nationally acclaimed movie about her life as a Mathematician at the Center. Although this was a different environment for me, I felt comfortable. After completing my assignments, I would frequently assist the teachers in correcting papers and tutoring students. I enjoyed the work I was doing and seeing my initiative, the instructors gave me more responsibility and I started constructing practice entrance exam quizzes for the class. Because we were studying to pass the Federal Civil Service Entrance Examination, I used my smarts to develop a "mock" practice exam and became an "acting" teacher. I enjoyed this immensely. I had always wanted to be a teacher but my Mom told me I would end up hurting someone's child because of my lack of patience. I came to realize that teaching adults, rather than children, was my forte and I enjoyed every minute of it.

We took the Federal Civil Service Exam for Office Assistants that August and every one of the students passed. I passed with an 89.9 and was hired as a Clerical Trainee GS-1. My score qualified me to be placed in a GS-2 grade level position. I was hired February 1970 as a GS-1 Temporary Clerk-Typist Trainee. My assignment was to work with the primary teachers and the second Clerical Training Program that was about to begin. My primary duties were to correct papers, type and compose tests, teach arithmetic and basic typing principles. Teach typing, yeah! This was a big laugh for me, but I loved my job and looked forward to coming to work to do whatever I was assigned.

The clerical training program was quite unique and provided many benefits. When we began we were paid $1.60 per hour for 40 hours a week. We were given bus tokens to travel back and forth to the Air Force base. However, once I was hired and became a temporary employee, I was no longer eligible to receive free transportation. My husband had bought a little 1964 Karman Gia for me to drive to work. It was a stick shift and took more oil than gas. After I became a GS-1 conditional federal employee making $2.05 per hour or $4,125 a year, I purchased my first car from the local Ford dealership. I wanted a Ford Mustang, but it was $99 a month and I could not afford that, so I got a baby blue Ford Maverick for $79 a month. I was so happy that I had bought my first brand-new car! My boys and I took our first drive to North Carolina almost as soon as I drove off the lot and enjoyed every mile.

I was blessed to have two these powerful women mentoring me. The primary instructor was quiet, yet straight-forward in her dealings with people. Her assistant was a bit more outgoing and "flighty" but was a sweetheart. She and her husband lived privileged lives. I believe he was an attorney and they lived in a house near the water. Money did not seem to be a problem for them. She said she saw a lot of potential in me and asked if I wanted to go to college. I responded with a resounding "yes" and she jump-started my college education by paying for my first college course at the local community college! Books and fees included. I was ecstatic. I always wanted to go to college but I could not afford it with my meager salary and we only had my husband's income and he wasn't thinking about sending me to college. I was looking forward to this new experience where I could learn more and get a college degree. My primary instructor was concerned with my grammar and public speaking. She reminded me I would be expected to be articulate to move up in the ranks in the government. Without really saying it, she was saying as a black female you would be expected to speak proper English and enunciate clearly, or as I would say, "speak white." Therefore, she enrolled me in the local Toastmasters Program to help me develop my speaking skills. I caught on fairly quickly and was feeling really good about my improvement. I had a habit of saying "okay" after every few words and this program helped me first identify the habit, then armed with this I was able to stop the annoying habit. I enjoyed my Toastmasters Program and even started a class later in my career.

This was not the only class I attended. My instructors sent me to several Office of Personnel Management classes offered by the Civil Service Commission. I enjoyed meeting other people working for the government and learned a lot about the way the system worked. Now remember, I was still assigned as a GS-1 Clerical Trainee but was performing at a higher grade as a Training Instructor. I was promoted a few months later to a GS-2 Clerical Trainee with the same duties. So, I began the quest to determine how to get that changed. This required some extra studying, which was not a problem for me. I started with the federal personnel regulations regarding position titles, promotions, and qualifications. I even enrolled in correspondence courses on these topics I could take on my own.

I was becoming more visible to management. My teachers, the Training Department Director, and the Personnel Director all commented about my potential to perform at a higher grade level. Although I was waiting to see the results of what they were saying put into action, I continued to read and study the regulations to enhance my knowledge about the federal personnel system. It was going to be very interesting to see how I would progress to the grade I deserved for the work I was performing.

As the second Clerical Training Program class was finishing, the entire program was transferred to the Training Office of the Personnel Division. One of the other trainees who was placed at the same time as I was had been assigned to the Training Office as the Administrative Assistant to the Training Director. The Training Director was a man of God. He loved people and did whatever he could to increase hiring and promotions among the minority population. He made sure the woman assigned to his office was given periodic awards and promotions for her performance. He had a lot of faith in the future of the program and was pleased to have it under his department.

Within a year of my assignment with the clerical training program, the two primary teachers left the program and I became the only primary teacher. Later I was given the authority to hire an assistant to work with me. That December 1970, almost ten months later, I received my first financial award. It was a sustained superior performance award for the effectiveness of the Clerical Training Program and the next month I was promoted to a GS-3 permanent career employee. Little steps toward that higher grade were beginning to materialize.

A workshop for agency supervisors and managers was being held in Florida. Because our program was so effective in diversifying the clerical workplace, the Training Office sent me to brief the attendees on our program. I was ecstatic! This was my first flight! I was so giddy, I took pictures of the clouds, my hotel room, the outside of the hotel and everything I could. I loved taking pictures and this would document my adventures when I got the chance to share my adventure with the family later. When it was my time to brief, I was a little nervous because this auditorium was full of people, mostly white, but I squared my shoulders and stood straight. I thought about my instructor and silently thanked her for ensuring I would be prepared for these types of situations. I proudly shared how our Center had developed this process to identify, train and hire the under-skilled for permanent clerical positions. I proudly pointed out I too was a graduate of the program. The information was well received and people stood and clapped. There was an African American woman who stood up in the back row and asked me a question. I had not seen her before. She wanted to know my grade. I gladly responded that I was a GS 3– Personnel Clerk. She gasped! By the time I returned to my Center, I was surprised to see on my desk a Personnel Action form promoting me from the GS-3 to a GS-5 Training Assistant (Clerical) signed personally by the Center Director. I was amazed especially since I had been told you couldn't skip grades unless the occupational series was a two graded interval. I believe that woman was instrumental in making this happen and I often wonder who she was! My love for helping the teachers, correcting papers, and tutoring the students paid off as my title was changed and I began to be recognized for the job I was doing. Things were changing. Guess that potential was paying off!

As I was progressing in my career with the federal government, my family continued to be incredibly supportive and helped me with my boys. I do not know what I would have done without the help of my mama, Mother-in-law, youngest sister, and family friends who kept the kids while I worked and went to school. This truly depicts what "it takes a village" to raise kids looks like.

Currently, many of the African American pioneers at the Center are being recognized for their contributions to the space program. Some that were not mentioned were the many clerical trainees who graced the Center with their presence as Clerks after completing the Clerical Training Program. I personally salute all these ladies for making the crack in the clerical ceiling at the Center that allowed young under educated, under-privileged women of color the opportunity to gain employment that would have a lasting impact on their lives, their families and their communities. Many of them went on to have successful careers with the federal government and have since retired. We were there!

STEPPING DOWN TO STEP AHEAD

Soon after my promotion at the Center, my husband received orders to return to North Carolina. He wanted us to join him and although I didn't want to leave my great job and wonderful supervisors, however, I started looking for a job there. Because I was a military spouse the federal government allowed me priority placement at my spouse's duty location. I found a job in the Personnel Department but it meant I would have to take a down-grade. I called and talked with the hiring officials and was given the assurance that although I would take a down-grade, I would not lose any pay. My pay would be adjusted to what I was making at the higher grade. I took a GS-3 Personnel Clerk position. Within one year I was back up to my GS-5 position and was assigned to the Training Department. Nobody but God!!

This time when we went to North Carolina, we purchased a house. It cost us $17,000. It was a beautiful rancher with 3 bed-rooms and a bath and a half. It sat on a large corner lot and we had lots of yard in the back, on the side and front. My husband even planted a garden in the back. Things were going well. The kids liked their school and I was getting used to the people in the Personnel office. However, my husband and I started arguing more and more. Our marital issues began again. One day a neighbor called me at work to tell me there was a party going on at my house in the middle of the work day. I left my job and came home to find people in my house having a party. I asked them all to leave and of course my husband was upset. His father had given me a rifle and told me to use it when needed. I decided this was one of those times although I didn't shoot anyone, I pulled it out and fired it. I was done and determined not to take this anymore!! I took leave from my job, packed up my sons and we moved back to my hometown in Virginia.

Our return to Virginia took us back to my parent's house for a short while until our apartment became available. The apartment was down the sidewalk from my parents and younger siblings who were still at home. I immediately checked the federal job listings and found a position at the local Army post. My last position in North Carolina was as a GS-5, Employee Development Specialist. I was accepted for a position as a GS-5 Personnel Assistant in the installation command where I worked for about a year. A job was advertised for a Training Technician working with the military assigning school quotas to soldiers for military schools. I thought this sounded interesting, so I applied. It was a GS-6 position, so it would be a promotion. During the interview the Major was very impressed with my pursuing school while continuing to raise my three sons as a single Mom. When we were in North Carolina, I continued to take classes from the local Technical college and even started teaching English as a Second Language classes. The Major said those magical words that I had heard most of my career, "you have a lot of potential" so he hired me for the job although I had not worked for the military before in that capacity. Most of the jobs I had held were working with civilians so this was a switch. I was able to learn the regulations and apply the system effectively and efficiently.

I suggested some changes which were implemented and made the application of school quotas work more smoothly. I was awarded my first Military Certificate of Appreciation and a military medal for my performance.

My sons and I continued to be close and although we had a difficult family life, we still had each other. We spent many hours having discussions sitting around the kitchen table. These discussions ranged from what was going on in their schools, to updates on the latest family happenings, dreams of our next "road trip" adventure as well as where we would live when we grew up. Now at 27, I was only a few years older than them - they were 10, 9 and 8 (I was 17 when my first son was born) and I felt we were tackling some of the same issues. What did I want to do with the rest of my life? Where would I live? What subjects would I continue to study in school? Did I want to work and continue to go to school? I had finally gotten pass a GS-5 grade level and out of the clerical field.

It was again time for a change. I applied for a job outside of my current occupational specialty in a totally different occupation. The position I applied for would require me to take a down-grade from a GS-6 Training Technician to go to a GS-5 Equal Opportunity (EO) Specialist. I knew I would not lose any money, so I decided to take the risk. Going into this new field was a little scary for me because I did not have a full grasp of the military administrative regulations. Most of my positions had been in offices with civilians. This would be my first assignment working directly with only a military staff. I was excited about the challenge of the new venture. My new job required me to listen to and advise commanders and soldiers about issues relating to discrimination. I didn't know many military members or the types of issues they were confronted with in performing their jobs. Therefore, I sought advice from the Post Sergeant Major. He told me first of all I had to gain the trust of the soldiers if they were going to come to me with their issues. He said the best way to do that was to go where they went. Well, most of the enlisted soldiers went to the club after work each day, so I made that an extension of my office time. It worked! The more soldiers saw me out in certain places, the more confident they became that I could be trusted. I started visiting the squadrons and companies to have coffee with the senior leaders and began to develop relationships with them. I gained their trust as well as someone that was a straight shooter. They felt confident I would tell them the truth about issues being faced by their soldiers that may impact readiness.

A short time after beginning the EO position, I was selected to attend a 16-week training program in Florida at the premier training agency that certified equal opportunity personnel. This training impacted my life in a number of ways. I made a decision to focus my federal career on pursuing equal opportunity occupations. Counseling military members was only one aspect of the career field. Training was a major component. The training we took covered some very touchy emotional areas. It was mostly sensitivity training and some people, especially senior enlisted and officers became very uncomfortable discussing these issues. The training was focused on changing attitudes, not just behaviors. Changing behaviors was safe, but when we talked about changing attitudes that touched on one's values and beliefs and prejudices.

During my 16-week stay in Florida, my sons stayed with my family. On the first day of the orientation at the training agency, the Commandant, a female Navy Commander, stated they had not had much success with civilian students and she didn't think that I would make it. What did she say that for? At that very moment, I made up my mind that I would graduate and be in the top percentile of the class.

The training was very intense and taught me some things about myself that I did not know. It ended up being life changing. I met some really nice and caring people. All the members of the class were active duty and reserve military members of different ethnic groups and genders, and I was the only civilian. We worked together in small groups to address the issues that were put before us. This class caused me to address some of my prejudices and embrace a new concept of real love. We had not grown up with much physical love being shown in our home so to say that we were love starved would be on point. I had not told my sons regularly how much I loved them. I knew my parents loved me, but to say it was not something that they had grown up with so they didn't speak of their love for us. This was one of the changes that I implemented in my family when I returned. I started hugging! I encouraged my parents to hug us and I started hugging my sons more. My Dad was a bit uncomfortable with the hugging but he did anyway. I started saying "I love you" and encouraged them to do the same. It made such a difference. We all accepted that we were loved, but to hear it meant so much.

Some of the people I met had deep seated prejudices. Our classroom was directly across the street from the Ocean. One day during an intensive pulling back the cover session regarding prejudices, one of my team mates walked out headed across the street to the ocean. I caught up with him and asked him where he was going and he said he didn't want to live any longer now that he had come face to face with the prejudice and the discriminatory behaviors his family had taught him. I was able to talk him out of walking into the ocean and from that day forward, I became aware of how serious these deep-seated attitudes could be. He was a white Navy sailor from a Mid-Western state. Because I had come to grips with some of my own prejudices, I was feeling more and more convinced about making this my choice of a career field knowing the number of people I would be able to help.

We studied together, cried together, partied together and passed our requirements. On graduation day, I was in the top 10 percent of the class and felt great about my accomplishments. I would never forget this life changing experience.

I returned to the Army post and continued my work in EO and received a promotion to a GS-7. Within about four months I got a call from some friends at the Air Base in Florida to inform me the EO Officer position for the Air Force Base that was coming open. I was told to apply for the job because the base was looking for a change. I had made an impression on some folks at the school while I was there for the 16-week training. My involvement with the base was minimal, but there were some positive comments made about my involvement. Because of the school's influence on the base, I went ahead and submitted my package for the GS-9, not really sure that I would qualify. I was rated eligible and selected. Florida here we come!

VISIONS DO MANIFEST

As the boys and I prepared for our relocation to Florida, we envisioned what our Florida home would look like. It would have at least 4 bedrooms, spacious yards to entertain our large family, a spacious kitchen and dining area and of course a comfortable living room. I also wanted a "Florida room" where we could have our music racks and lots of sunlight. This would be the first time the boys had their own rooms, so the testosterone was freely flowing as they tried to outwit each other. As we visualized what we wanted our space to look like, I assured them that if they could believe it and see it, they we could have it. My relationship with God was not very strong during those days and I did not give God his rightful place in this scenario. However, those are some of the reasons today that I thank God for not letting my lack of relationship with Jesus impact the blessings he bestowed upon us. I did not fully seek Him first, but I did give Him the glory at the end. Of course, I knew He was involved in this entire process because it could not have happened the way it did without His intervention. Later I repented of this self-serving behavior. Thank God he forgives us! Not just 70 times 7 as he calls us to do with our brother, but He has forgiven me so many times more than those 490 times.

The first house the real estate agent found for us did not meet all the criteria we had envisioned, but because I was ready to settle down, I decided we would take it and make the best of it. Up pops a bank denial. We could not get the house because of some financial qualification issue. I was a little frustrated because I had painstakingly taken care of all the details I believed, would be necessary to guarantee approval for the house. I was a single parent now and only my salary was considered in the purchase of the home. However, I had not owned a house with only my name before. The house in North Carolina was jointly owned. I felt I had been slapped across the face when the bank denied me. I was fixated on having our own space. We were living with a friend I met while at the training school and I felt we were becoming a burden and wearing out our welcome. There were some personality issues and other behaviors that were not totally acceptable. That is another story for another time and title!

But God worked it out. Within about three weeks, we experienced the meaning of the Scripture, "God will work it all out for the good of those who love him and are called according to his purpose." The realtor found the house we had visualized. We made application and everything passed with flying colors and we even had some money left. I pridefully thought this was the result of great financial management on my part. After all I had learned to manage my finances quite well ever since I brought my first $25 leather coat as a pre-teen. Later I learned to repent for such thinking. These were experiences with God have taught me that He will give you the desires of your heart. Everything we had envisioned was in this house. These experiences attest to the overflow blessings that God continues to bring into my life. I have learned to give God the glory for every door he opened, window he shut and trial and tribulation that he brought me through!

After I surrendered to God, I took a look back over my life and saw how He had continually blessed me in situations like this and so many others. These and other incidents are a testimony to why I will bless the Lord at all times and his praise shall continue be in my mouth. He is such a good God and I cannot help but give him praise. Good is not even sufficient to describe how awesome God really was and is to us. Because of Him I found myself "unstoppable," not because of anything I did, but because of God. I thank God He did not knock me off my high horse before I realized I could do nothing, gain nothing, own nothing or even breathe without Jesus.

We loved our new home and the family came up from Virginia, Maryland and North Carolina to visit us. We were so happy to share our new home with them and we enjoyed our time together. The kids enjoyed their school. They walked to school or rode their bikes because it was not very far from where we lived. We lived in a predominately white neighborhood. We later found out there were people who lived around us who did not especially want us there. We became extra cautious about our movements and made friends in the neighborhood across from ours where more African American families lived. The boys would go there to play and I met a nice family and we became close friends. If I had to go out of town, I would leave the boys with my new friend and her family. She had boys and girls the same age as my children, so they enjoyed each other.

Florida is where my DJ past-time was born. I spent lots of time at the enlisted club and I befriended the local DJ. I told him of my love for music and about my music parties and suggested that he should let me DJ sometime. And he did!! I enjoyed this so much. There was a certain feeling I got standing behind that turntable and speaking into that microphone encouraging the people to just dance and let their troubles be gone, at least for the moment. I loved all kinds of music and started having music parties at my house. I would record music from various genres on my reel and then make cassette tapes from the reel and offer them to people for purchase. I had made lots of friends and had some great parties. We had so much fun at these music parties and they became a regular way for us to unwind. I met a nice guy who became a good close friend. He lived not far from me in a trailer and we had some great times together. He was in the Air Force and helped me understand a lot more about the military. When his Mom and Dad came to visit, I got a chance to meet them. They were very nice and really loved their only child. Our relationship ended when I moved to Germany although we remain in contact today.

MOBILITY

My Florida assignment was quite exciting and lead to some other life changing behaviors. My marriage relationship had not survived the separation. But one day I got a message that my husband was sick and at the the Medical Hospital in Washington DC. The boys and I went to see him and asked if he would like to come back home with us to Florida to recuperate. He agreed, so we brought him back to Florida with us. Things started out really good. The boys had not been around their father for many years. He was recuperating and we enjoyed having him around. After his convalescent period ended, he received orders to go to Germany. He asked if we would go with him. This was a major decision. This would be our first time living outside of the country. The boys and I talked about how things might be, aware that we would not be able to see the family very often. We may even have to learn a foreign language, German, so we could get around in the country. I was asking the guys to think long and hard about this decision. I think I was more concerned about me than them because once I said yes, I couldn't just jump up and leave when things didn't go right. I hadn't completely surrendered, so my issues were still alive. We agreed to give it a try thinking maybe being in a different country would help our family. I had no intentions of going without being able to find a job and have my own income. I did some research in advance to ensure I would be able to continue my government career in Germany. I wasn't ready to leave my new home in Florida or the job that I enjoyed, my friends or my new found freedom, but I was willing to give it a try.

We were married on paper for 25 years. Five of those years were spent in Germany. I can count a total of 10 years that we actually lived together. In the beginning our separations were due to his duty assignments. But because of our continual marital problems and separations, I started looking for positions based on my own federal career status. My mobility was a plus and allowed me to relocate for different positions with the government. We moved quite a bit over the 20 years of his military assignments and my subsequent federal positions. We lived in three different states: Virginia, Florida, North Carolina and one foreign country: Germany. We lived in Virginia and North Carolina on three separate occasions. Life was complicated but manageable. Being the wife of a military spouse had its advantages and disadvantages. The fact we could expect to move about every three years or so was a plus. After what seems like the hundredth time of our separations, the boys and I prepared for another move.

Moving not only presents opportunities to meet new people, but it also opens up employment opportunities. I remember when I was in North Carolina, the federal agency had an Upward Mobility Program. People who were enrolled in the program had to sign an agreement that they would move at the end of their training. I thought this was a great program and many young, unmarried people took advantage of it. Moving allows a person to leave the drama of past relationships behind and begin anew in a different place. Some people do not like moving, are reluctant to make new friends, or fear they will not meet friends like the ones they had before. Not us, we looked forward to the moves knowing that there would always be a new adventure. I guess my sons and I were all "free spirits" and ready for new challenges.

When I asked my oldest son what he thought about the frequent moves he said he found moving a plus in that it exposed them to different cultures and ethnicities. He said if they had not moved, they would have probably been in the same neighborhood, seeing the same things and people and becoming a product of the environment. Although it was always fun to come home back home to Virginia for visits, living in different places was really fun and helped him see things from different perspectives. When you have been exposed to lots of things you have more information upon which to make decisions.

My free-spirited middle son would rather show then tell and at 15 years old he did just that. The first day we arrived in Germany he left the house and went off the post without letting us know where he was going. I was scared to death he would get lost or something worse since he did not know anyone, speak the language nor did he know his way around. He returned after a few hours with this great big smile and five different ethnically different teenage boys. None of them spoke English! He wanted us to meet his new friends and tell us that he had caught the train with them and had gone to McDonalds. From that day forward, I knew he would become a European replant. During the time he was in Europe, he spent time in Africa, many states in Germany and who knows where else. He still lives there and has been a part of that culture longer than he spent time in America. Sometimes talking to him he has to stop to remember the American word because he speaks and thinks in German.

I always looked forward to changing jobs. Oftentimes there was a promotion with the job change and that was always a welcome occurrence especially since most of resources used to raise the boys came from my employment. Relocations offered me the opportunity to learn new skills and use them to make an impact in the workplace and my family. I always looked forward to the challenge that came with developing new skills. It was never a solitary pursuit. When assigned as the Training technician allocating slots for advanced military training, I sought out the most knowledgeable person in the office to help me. I put in the extra hours and took books home to brush up on these specialties and become acquainted with the nomenclature. After a short while on this job, I was allocating training spaces and filling classes at the most efficient rate ever achieved. Being mobile allowed me to move from this position to many positions in the EO field at various camps and stations within the military and other federal agencies outside of the defense department.

NEED TO ACHIEVE

The need to achieve was my driving force and words of affirmation always made me want to do more. There was a force within me that drove me to believe I could accomplish anything I chose to do. *I was unstoppable!* Learning and retaining knowledge were always easy for me. My Mother often related how I didn't do much homework, but that I always brought home good grades. This continued on into my adult years. It was a gift. My Mom told me that when I was little, my father would read me a book or something from the newspaper and I would repeat what he had told me from memory. She said I would hold a book upside down and repeat everything my father had read as if I were reading the book. I loved my Daddy and really wanted him to know that I was listening and could remember what he said. In elementary school she said I got good grades and she never saw me doing much studying.

During my federal career, I seized any opportunity I was offered to attend any type of training. Another very challenging program that I was selected to attend after about 15 years as a new federal program manager, was the Army Management Staff College. Its curriculum fostered a total person approach to management - physical, intellectual, emotional, and spiritual. I had to study to pass the intellectual tests and spend countless hours taking care of my physical body in order to satisfy the physical tests while at the same time not getting emotionally distraught. To be honest, the physical requirements were tougher than the intellectual part. This was the first experience of this type I had and it required a lot of effort. I trusted God to give me the spiritual strength I needed to make it through this challenging, yet fun program.

This was a great challenge and again I held a one-of-a-kind position as the only Black female civilian in my class. I determined I would excel. My achievements resulted in a life-sized cardboard picture of me being placed on the wall in the command auditorium. It was intended as a symbol to encourage other civilians attending the program, especially, black females. These types of learning opportunities were always in my future, and I was inspired by the new challenges. The more challenges the more opportunities to achieve.

PLANNING

God laughs every time we make our plan. I could not have planned my life to go the way it did. In the early days of my life, I knew "about" God, but I did not really "know" God. As such, I made my plans and had the audacity to ask God to bless them. After all, I was a smart woman who had had a lot of success in the plans I had made.

My life was earmarked by one plan after another. I was on the move and not just surviving. I chose to be unstoppable and to accomplish all that I could during the time God had given me. A plan that went awry ended up contributing to one of my fondest memories. The Air Force Office where I worked in Florida provided services in alcohol and drug and the equal opportunity and treatment areas. It served many tenants on the base as well as Geographically Separated Units which were throughout the Caribbean. It was a highly visible installation because of its location along the Ocean coastline and a place where many senior officials came to vacation. I was planning to go home for my 32d birthday that last weekend of March. I was faithfully finishing my monthly reports so I could get on the highway that Friday. I got a call that was about to alter my plans. I was told to report to the Center Commander's office right away. He informed me of a human relations situation occurring in

Antigua between American and Antiguan blacks. He related to me that my services were required in Antigua immediately to handle the situation which could become volatile if not assessed and resolved. My birthday weekend plans had to be cancelled and I was booked to leave that day on the C130 Aircraft going to the island that I had no idea where it was or what it was. I was pissed! I would not be able to go home to spend my 32d birthday with my family. Not only was I going to miss my birthday with my family, I would not be taking a commercial flight to Antigua, but the Colonel said he had a special seat reserved for me on this cargo plane. I had never flown on a military cargo plane before and did not know what to expect. However, I left his office steaming and went home to pack my bags and arrange for my children's care to fly off on a cargo plane to some island.

This plane was huge and designed to carry cargo, not passengers! We sat with our backs toward the pilot instead of facing the cockpit as you would on a commercial flight. The ride was bumpy and I even barfed in the bags that they had been especially provided for that purpose. I didn't have a window to look out of so I didn't know what to expect when the plane landed. But the moment we deplaned, I beheld one of the most beautiful sites I had ever seen. The white sand and beautiful blue water left me breathless. My emotional anger subsided. What would have been a birthday weekend in Virginia was going to be a memorable celebration in a Caribbean paradise!

My stay was amazing. I had never been out of the country before and especially to such a beautiful place. The assignment ended up being an exciting week which was extended to another week. My Chief came to Antigua to lend a hand in the resolution and felt we needed just a few more days to ensure everything was resolved. I had applied the skills I had learned during my first EO job where the Sergeant Major advised me to go where the soldiers went if I wanted to interact with them. I found that a local community bar was where both the Antiguans and Americans hung out and I went there. Shooting darts was the favorite pastime, so I quickly learned to shoot darts, and became pretty good at it. The local people where welcoming, personable, communicative, and quite laid back. The situation was resolved early during my visit as I had taken the time to develop relationships and get to know the people and their values. As Americans working alongside the locals, we were often viewed as showing superior behavior and warranting special treatment. My observations during this visit revealed that non-American blacks perceived American blacks as boastful, pretentious and arrogant. The Americans were bragging about their possessions and standard of living as compared to the native peoples. This belief and behavior resulted in strained relationships between the two groups of people who, although the same color, had different value systems. After some training and relationship building around the dart boards at the local community bar, we were able to resolve the differences. We walked away with everyone accepting that they had the same desires to earn a living, care for their families and enjoy life. The locals laid back "don't worry, be happy, no stress man" attitude was better understood by the Americans who learned that relationships were just as important as getting the task completed. What I believed was going to be a disruption to a birthday celebration with family will always stand out as one of my fondest memories. This beautiful paradise was implanted in my mind and I think this contributed to my insatiable desire later on to take cruises to the Caribbean Islands every chance I got.

LIFE IN GERMANY

We left Florida after about two years and were reunited as a family in Germany where we remained for five years, although our orders were for three years. However, each year we extended our stay to allow our sons to complete their high school years at the American High School. Our three boys were in middle school when we went to Germany. As it happened each year when we were up for rotation, one of the boys was preparing to graduate. We didn't want to bring them back to the states and have them start over their last year in High school, consequently, we would extend our stay in Germany. Their graduations were for three consecutive years. It may have been a challenge for my military man with the field duties and other uncomfortable situations he encountered, but we took advantage of the many travel opportunities and enjoyed life in this foreign country as much as we could.

The installation had a Youth Activities Program that focused on providing outreach activities and events for the youth assigned to the post. I became a program volunteer so whenever there was a trip, I could chaperone the youth. Since my three sons were usually on these trips, it was a no brainer for me. They were very visible because we were the only family with three African American teen-aged boys on the post. So anytime any youth mischief occurred, we were the first ones interviewed. Just to keep my eyes on them and have first-hand knowledge of their behavior, I would take leave from my job and go on their trips. I enjoyed each trip because it gave me the opportunity to see more of Europe. Although my spouse didn't like to travel, he never objected to me and the boys taking trips.

One of the few trips we took as a couple was when he went with me on a boat trip to Sweden to pick up the Saab I had purchased. We drove the car back from the port in Bremerhaven to our quarters in Dudenhofen. It was such a beautiful ride and the countryside was pristine. The Germans had the cleanest streets and communities I had ever seen. Most of the cars in Germany were Mercedes and BMWs. We had owned a Mercedes and 7 Series BMW and this Saab handled well on the highway. The Autobahn was the highway system in Germany and in many places, there were no speed limits. I always loved to drive and driving my Saab was an enjoyable new experience. She proved to be a fun and fulfilling experience on our girls rode trip to Belgium later that month.

I made some life-long friends while we were in Germany. Life in a foreign country was different. Americans freely gathered together because we all had something in common, we were all a long way from home and shared a common nationality. It didn't matter what your color or ethnicity was, you were American and that was the common thread that drew us together. Our living quarters were on the German economy in the designated military high rise buildings. We quickly learned to depend on each other and look out for each other. Although we went out into the community to shop and befriend our German neighbors, there were was nothing like our homies. One of the ladies I met was also experiencing her first time in a foreign country, far away from family. She was a new military wife and had one daughter. We quickly became friends and helped each other adjust to the military life away from family and friends at home. She is still a great friend today and we continue to be extended family.

Another one of my best friends was my administrative assistant. One of my jobs in Germany was that of a Family Day Care administrator. I was responsible for the in-home child care programs on the base. I hired a docile, yet talented female from her volunteer position at the Red Cross to work with the program. I later found out she was not a typist, but was very creative which was helpful in developing our marketing materials, handbooks and learning materials for the child care program. She had two young children, a girl and a boy. Her husband was very protective of her and preferred she spend her time at home. She too had never lived outside of the United States and was getting used to being a military spouse. My outgoing personality and "control" encouraged her to join me and my family and others in experiencing some of Germany. We went to the "Gasthaus," the local restaurant and bar, and took lots of driving trips exploring the surrounding towns and villages. She fell in love with Germany and before long her frequent absences from home led to her separation from her husband. As a result, she returnd to the states. She took her daughter with her and her husband insisted that their son remain in Germany with him. She became one of my best friends and we made lots of memories while we were in Germany. When she returned to the states, I went to Arizona to help her set up her ceramics business. We traveled throughout the beautiful mountains in Sedona and went to the Grand Canyon and just enjoyed life. She and her daughter became a very important part of my family. Her son and husband returned to Florida from Germany and we remain in touch with each other. We spent a lot of time together reminiscing about our travel and time in Germany. She loved coffee and wine and so did I. Everywhere we went we always had our coffee pot (and pot) and a bottle of wine. We remained friends until the end when that cancer demon took her from us in 2019. She will always hold a special place in my heart as a true friend.

Living in Germany was a major contributor to my family's current geographical separation. We learned that we could travel the world yet still maintain the closeness we had developed as a family. We all decided we would live in different states and countries so we would have different places to visit. That is exactly what happened! Take this warning from me, when you ask God for something; please be prepared to receive it. My family is now global, and we live in three countries and three different states. My number two son, his wife and my grand-daughter and step grand-son live in Germany. My oldest son's daughter and my great-grandson live in South Korea while his son, my grand-son and great-grand daughter, live in California. My former daughter-in-law and step grand-daughters live in Italy. My number three son, his wife and my grand-daughter live in Arizona. My number one son relocated to Virginia after he and his wife spent some time in North Carolina.

There was a cost to all this global living. I was not able to be with my grandkids or great-grands as much as they were growing up. I was not involved in many of their experiences. Yes, we stay in touch through the internet and its social media tools, but the physical absence cannot be replaced by electronics. We were raised as a close family and we enjoyed traveling so we looked forward to the fun we would have traveling to different places to visit each other. Of course, one little area we overlooked was "who would pay for the transportation to these places!" Nonetheless, we traveled and made the best of our lives. We made the choice to be unstoppable!

FIGHT OR FLIGHT

My ability to resolve others differences ought to be a helpful tool in resolving issues I faced in my life. I spent many years helping to resolve others conflicts but was continually haunted by my own inner battles. Why should I feel discouraged? How could this continue to plague me? I thought I had gotten rid of this "depression" the last time it attacked me. What is going on? Every time I think I have conquered this demon; he shows up again with a vengeance. What is the root cause of this? Why do I continue to repeat the same things I know do not contribute to my growth? It is true, as a person thinks, so does he become. My mind gets me in trouble. If you think long enough and focus enough on a thing it really will materialize. I have first-hand experience with how to deal with situations that appear to be distasteful. I refer to it as fight or flight!

My early days in the federal government were unbridled with the concept of fight or flight. I was frequently unsatisfied and not content. Not just with the salary or job duties, I just wanted more. I felt that I could perform the duties of every supervisor I had ever been assigned. As a result, I often became frustrated because I found myself doing my supervisors' jobs while they relaxed or whatever and got the pay! When they allowed me to perform a great amount of their duties, the results were always superior and I always made my supervisors look good. Inadvertently they permitted me to satisfy my need to achieve. The benefit to me was the additional knowledge, skills, and abilities I gained which made my resume more attractive. My frustration was self-imposed. I can truly see now it all stimmed from my need to control things. Being in control required building relationships, exercising patience with people and showing genuine love. All of these were still areas of growth for me. I was not focused on my shortcomings, because I was too busy focusing on what someone else was not doing to actually look in the mirror at myself. Oftentimes, I would over-look a situation I deemed as stressful just to maintain my sanity. I was always looking for the next job opportunity, so I frequently told myself I could stand and fight for a little while longer.

Job opportunities were continually on my radar. I made it a practice of checking out the potential job sites when I could, even before applying for the job. I availed myself of every opportunity I could to put my paperwork in the "hopper" for the next job opportunity. It was not always a promotion, sometimes I took downgrades just to get into another career field. I did my due diligence. Going to the jobsite before- hand helped me get a feel of the work environment. Visiting the job site and talking to people at the site was always helpful and was a part of my application process. I needed to like the place as much as they would like to hire me to work with them. I checked to see what people wore to work. The office attire was a key to blending. If people wore business casual, I did not want to be too casual or too formal. So, these pre-visits helped me to prepare myself for the interview. I believed if I looked like I already worked there, that is, blended in with everyone, the chances of my being hired would improve. This was helpful to my fight or flight syndrome.

My final flight from the federal government came soon after 9-11 in 2001. I was working as the Diversity Program Director at the headquarters in Washington DC for this great federal agency that served the needs of people throughout the world. I was conducting a week-long Equal Opportunity counselors training for a group of students from overseas and state-side offices. The incident on that fatal Tuesday in September made me realize how vulnerable our country was. I had never seen such chaos in my entire life and I decided at that moment it was time for me to leave the government. I contacted Human Resources and had them work up my retirement figures. I was told I would have to take a six percent reduction because I had not reached the age of 55 although I had the 30 years of service. I prayed about it, did the math and realized my transportation, clothing, daily food and other job-related spending would compensate for the reduction. At the end of September, I said farewell to my colleagues. This was final fight. I was sick of fighting the government bureaucracy so I took an early flight out.

My retirement from the federal government at the top GS rank was such a blessing and a personal achievement. I am thankful every day that I was able to stay long enough to complete a career with the federal government. I am thankful that God gave me the home I asked for during my early years living in North Carolina. Instead of gold fish swimming in the pond, I have an entire lake of fish! I am thankful for being able to use my gift of teaching to impact others. My continual prayer is that God will "fix me" and help me to become the woman he has purposed me to be. My desire is to be patient and trust His plan which is so much greater than mine. I have always been a "Type A" personality, one who will make it happen, but I have learned that sometimes making it happen is not the will of God. I have learned waiting on God means trusting Him to do what He wills, when He wills. Consequently, this demon of impatience that continually hangs around me is like the thorn in Paul's side that reminds him as stated in 2 Corinthians 12:9, "His grace is sufficient and his power works best in weakness."

I returned to Virginia in 2002, a year after retirement, to assist the newly assigned young pastor at my home church. This was another situation that I thought would become a fight or flight dilemma. This move was not part of "my plan." My Mother informed the new pastor that her daughter had just retired from the government and could come help him with the church. That day a prophetic Word was spoken. Well, after requesting release from my awesome Pastor and my great church in Maryland, I returned to Virginia, yet again.

Little did I know that I had been in preparation for this next journey. My church in Maryland had an awesome Bible Institute and the classes that were offered prepared you to function in the Gospel ministry. I had started taking ministerial classes at my Maryland church. I never really wanted to be a preacher. I wanted to be a teacher and teach the Word of God. I had experienced some not so pleasant interactions in the past with a few preachers that left a bad taste in my mouth, so I did not want to follow that path. I did however, love the Word of God and loved the teaching I had done with the government, so this was my opportunity to gain more knowledge and become better prepared to teach the Word. But I still was reluctant to take on the title of preacher. After consulting with our Assistant Pastor, I was informed that you cannot be a preacher if you are not able to teach. So, I continued to take the ministerial classes and shifted my focus on gaining more knowledge to be a minister, in whatever capacity God could use me.

My life changed dramatically while I was at my Maryland church. It became very clear later that this was the place God had used to equip me for my next assignment. I met this man who I thought was going to be my second husband. He invited me to come to his church when we met one Saturday night at a club. I wasn't really sure he was sincere, but after I met his Mom, who was wheel-chair bound and his sister, I began to feel more comfortable. They were really sweet and his Mom and I developed a great relationship. My boy-friend was very nice and I believe I fell in love. He loved music like I did and we enjoyed many of the jazz concerts that came to the area. He liked to dance and we went out dancing often. He also liked to cook, so I was happy about that and willingly gave up the kitchen. We would have long conversations about life and our goals that would last late into the night.

He commuted from his sister's house in Maryland where he was living to Virginia to see me. He worked odd jobs and was trying to get enough funds together to get his own place. His sister and her family had taken him in but he was ready to move. Because he was spending so much time at my apartment in Virginia, I invited him to stay over and sleep in my second bedroom. Later we agreed that he would move in with me, but still sleep in the second bedroom. Well, that did not last long before we found ourselves tipping to each other's rooms at night. I was feeling convicted about our relationship but continued to tell myself that he would be my husband one day and it was okay with God. I took him home to meet the family and everyone liked him, except my Mom. She said there was something about him that was not right. Take my advice LISTEN TO YOUR MOM.

As time went on, I learned my boy-friend had a serious drug problem. One year I bought him a Gucci watch for his birthday.

When I asked where it was, he would tell me he did not want to wear it to work so he left it at his sister's house. A few months later I found out he had sold the watch to buy drugs. We talked about his addiction and he agreed to enroll in a Christian drug rehabilitation program where he lived for a few months. Once he was released, we continued our relationship. But within six months, he was back to using drugs and went back into the program. This time he told me that I wasn't good for him and he did not want to continue our relationship. I was devastated! This man, who I thought I loved and would be my next husband, was kicking me to the curve. It took me many days and nights to get over this. I had never felt like this before and it was a terrible feeling. I wanted to take flight and get as far away from this place as I could. But I had my church, so I confessed, repented and asked God to restore me and give me another chance to get it right. And of course, he did. My friend was very active in the church and had a great support group there. He later married another older woman from the church and life for them began and ended in separation. However, he was never really able to shake that addiction. I don't know what took his life, but he was found a few years ago dead alone in his bed.

I thank God for my church. Although I was devastated, I continued my classes and let the Word heal me. Unstoppable! This was not the end. The Word of God continued to be taught and I took advantage of the conferences and seminars because I had developed an unquenchable hunger and thirst for the Word. I met a great group of women who were sold out for Christ and began meeting with their small group outside of church. They were an awesome part of my spiritual experience. They were led by an awesome woman of God who was my cosmetologist and also the sister of the man that

I thought I would marry. The Daughters taught me what it meant to really be sold out to a life in Christ. They were not ashamed of the gospel of Christ and were active in many ways in helping other young women face their demons and grow in their relationship with Christ. They asked me to be one of the women leaders, but in truth they were my example. They were always there whenever I needed them and they were so real in their Christian walk. They will always be a part of my life and I will forever remember how they helped me put both feet in the church and take one foot from out of the world. I learned through them that preaching may bring you out of the world, but teaching will bring the world out of you. Applying the Word to your everyday life is what it is all about.

I attended lots of classes at my church and it would take me one and half hours to get to class from my home in Virginia. I was going about three to four nights per week after working full time and commuting to work in DC about 45 minutes one-way per day. Nothing was going to stop me from learning more about this Christian walk. Eventually, I decided to move to Maryland to be closer and found a great house not very far from the church. As I continued my studies and was an integral part of the ministry, I was selected by the Dean of the Bible Institute to assist another teacher with his class. This was a great honor and privilege for me. He was a smart man although some of his beliefs were contrary to some of those taught by our pastor. I took my assignments seriously and did not allow his spirit to hinder me from gaining a greater knowledge of God. However, he did motivate me to study more diligently the Word of God and to be convinced about the Truth in my own mind.

This was my preparation. Armed with this enhanced knowledge of God, I came to my home church in Virginia. I had not taken my relationship with God seriously when I grew up there as a little girl, nor when I attended other churches as we moved around the world. Coming back home with a new relationship with Christ was going to be a very different experience. Within two years I was licensed as a minister and became the Church Administrator and Christian Education Director for the church. Two years later I was elevated to the position of Elder. From everything I had learned, a person who received the title Elder was supposed to be ready to take over a church or plant and grow their own church. I did not feel prepared for this assignment, but I accepted the challenge. God will not give you more than you can bear! Right!! Whom he calls he equips and whom he equips, he qualifies. This is what kept me encouraged on this new assignment. I knew this would be different from previous assignments, because I couldn't just take flight! I believed God was doing something in me and I wanted to accomplish whatever it was this time. No more running!

After I had been back at the church assisting the pastor for seven years, he decided he wanted to pursue other ministry opportunities and appointed me as his successor. I would not accept the position without the church voting to bring me on as their pastor. They voted me in! After understudying the pastor for seven years and serving as his right-hand person, I accepted the reigns as the first female pastor of a traditional Baptist church. That was a day I will never forget. I came home, lay across my bed and had a serious talk with God, asking Him if He was really sure that was what I was to do. I reminded God of my impatience with people, lack of understanding of why people failed to take responsibility, their unwillingness to grow in their relationship with Him and on and on. God just laughed!! He reminded me of how patient he had been with me. I was scared to death and just knew that God was up to something. After all, He allowed this to happen and could have stopped it at any time. I recall God reminding me that he would continue to prepare me as long as I was obedient and that He would be with me throughout the assignment. I resolved to trust Him. That was my song at my ordination service, "I Will Trust in the Lord." Little did I know how much that affirmation would play a major role in my life over the next few years as I came to realize my arms were really too short to box with God while my new assignment as Pastor of my home church began to unfold.

I saw people going through lots of struggles during the next few years. They wanted to live for God and keep His commandments, but it was a real struggle for many of them. Those who were not as mature in their relationship with God, learned about the grace and mercy of God and continued to live in sin knowing the grace and mercy of God would cover them. I took it personal!! And now, almost 10 years later, most of my time had been spent developing and teaching classes on basic biblical foundational truths. People attended the classes but there was little fruit being produced. The fruit that I observed did not show me that they had grown in their relationship with God. The comments about the classes were always positive. People continued to say they had learned so much more than they had ever learned before about the Bible and living a Christian life. I frequently asked God how could the teaching be so good and folks were learning more than they ever had before, yet there did not appear to be much change in their behavior? How could such blessed people not be willing to surrender themselves to God? I was not asking them to be perfect, no one on earth is. I felt their fruit should show more love for God and be exemplified by serving his people and loving each other.

I held on to this feeling for several years. The flight or fight syndrome was showing its head. I began to grow weary and asked God to release me from this assignment. I felt I had done all I could do. I believed they were content where they were and did not want to change and I was wasting my time. I knew there were people somewhere who wanted what I had to share. Their behavior did not reflect spiritual maturity as I felt it should, but each time I got frustrated God reminded me of my gift to teach and pray they would apply the principles to their lives. An answer came when I discovered I could use my mental energy to become a student at the Bible College and Seminary.

Two years after serving as the pastor, I enrolled in the college and seminary. My love for reading was definitely helpful as I undertook this arduous pursuit of a Doctor's in Ministry degree. Some of my colleagues thought I had lost it because I was a new pastor and was taking on the challenge of pursuing a doctor's degree. But no one knew this was really what saved my life and kept me from taking flight. The time I spent reading books, doing research and writing papers was the distraction I needed from what I believed to be the carnal Christians. My unstoppable nature would not allow me to start something and not finish it, so I put my all into my doctoral program.

Those two years of focused study were a God send. I was the new pastor in the class with three other seasoned pastors. My professor had been a pastor for over 25 years and had lots of stories to share. I learned so much from the others in the class and shared my limited pastoral knowledge. I later learned that my biblical knowledge

Jamie Bree

was highly respected by my class mates who were amazed at my understanding of the Word.

At the end of the two years of study, I submitted my 200-page dissertation for acceptance and approval. My dissertation was a model for my church and was titled "An Out of the Box Anointing" Growing the small urban church with a focus on reaching and retaining the postmodern generation. I had implemented much of what was included in my dissertation at my church. After graduation, I was asked to become a professor with the college and I accepted, yet another new challenge. As a Bible college and seminary professor for two years, I was able to help four people complete their Masters and Doctor's in Ministry degrees. God was still developing me as a pastor as I learned more and more about God and loving our neighbors as we love ourselves.

Because my motivational gift is teaching, I spent lots of hours researching and preparing classes and spiritual messages for my church. More times than not, I felt I was simply going through the motions. The reality was that I was focused on myself and would end up being frustrated and overwhelmed. I wanted to take flight and just quit. But I continually asked myself, "God is this assignment over?" All I ever heard was "just keep teaching." Keep your eyes on God and off the people. Remember what the Word of God says, some plant, some water, but God gives the increase. You may be planting, or watering, but when God is ready for them to grow, they will. I was being prideful and selfish, trying to be "Holy Ghost Junior" believing people should respond the way I wanted them to. Thank God he opened my eyes. But it took me dying to myself more and more every day. I am still in that dying process.

God's church and His people have been a blessing to me over

the past almost twenty years and have taught me to re-evaluate my tendency to fight or take flight. I have learned so much about people and God. He has taught me to always seek Him in everything I do and not to look to people for affirmation. This pastoral assignment is helping me to get control of my lack of patience and to learn to wait on the Lord for all things and while I wait, to continue to serve. The members of the church have grown in their spiritual relationship with God and it makes me proud to be able to say "it was in God's time, not mine." There have been quite a few people who came to the ministry and quite a few to leave, but the few that still remain are faithful and dedicated soldiers of God. When I realize the spiritual growth many of them are receiving, I get emotional. I began to see the plan unveil that God had for me all along. This plan included sharing my teaching gift with others, living a life before them that would honor him, accepting others where they are, being willing to wait on him and allowing him to take control of my life. It took this assignment for me to learn this lesson and God knew what it would take for me to finally get it. He knows each one of us. I feared Him enough to know I could not take flight this time, so I had to stand still and put on my armor and fight the good fight of faith.

MY THREE SONS

My sons and I have a great relationship and they all love me in their different ways. We have experienced some tuff times and they still respect me, seek my advice and proudly call me their Mom. They often speak about how much they appreciate the fact I never left them alone, always providing them a place to live, clothing and food. Times were not always as smooth as I may have wanted them to be, but we were unstoppable. Their father was not always there because of our differences, but I was determined to raise my sons the best that I knew how. Their father was strict and I had high expectations for them. Consequently, they were tainted with perfectionist expectations which impacted their adulthood. My infidelity in the marriage affected all of them as well as a lack of responsibility and control. All three of my sons chose to spend some time in the military whether they were following their father's footsteps or just saw it as a means to an end. They have married and all have children and lives of their own.

There is so much to say about my sons and I am not sure of what and how much to say. But just know as God has kept us all, including their Dad who remarried, became a widow and now is remarried again, God had a plan.

My oldest son is an articulate, intelligent, opinionated, powerful and extremely handsome 6 feet 3 inch 250 pound (as of this writing) black man who has endured lots of growing as a person and a black man. He chose a career in the Air Force but only served about two and a half years. His first marriage ended as a result of military separation and he and his daughter have an estranged relationship. He does not have a relationship with his grandson because of this and my continual prayer is that they both will humble themselves and forgive and experience the many blessings God has stored up for them. Because of a "date gone bad" he has had to deal with society's restraints for the past 20 years of his life. We are believing that the justice system will change and allow forgiveness to reign. He paid his dues but society is still holding him hostage. This is a constant reminder of how a decision to let the flesh rule will have devastating consequences that far out weight any pleasures you may receive. His second marriage ended due to pride and control and now he is experiencing a remake of the man. His philosophy now is to look at the man in the mirror and he has realized he does not always have the best answer to every situation. He is learning to trust God more and wait on his direction. Our relationship has overcome some trying downturns as he was going through self-discovery. Now we enjoy each other's company and can listen to each other's opinions without being confrontational. His dad used to say we were so much alike and that is why he had such personality clashess. We have both come to realize how true that is and have learned to respect each other's opinions. I am so proud of the man he is becoming and know God has great things in store for him.

My middle son has always been a free spirited, outgoing, life of the party guy. He is fun-loving and has a great heart. He was definitely made in the physical image of his father. He usually sees the best in people which has led to many upsets in his life. When we were first assigned to Germany, he went off exploring the very first day and returned with five new friends, all speaking a different language. Although we were scared out of our minds, I knew then that Europe would be appealing to him. He made friends easily and later joined the Army only to be stationed back in Germany. His military career did not last long, but he remained in Germany because of his connections with the entertainment community. He took a break from Europe and returned to the states after at least 15 years. He had overstayed his tourist Visa and was escorted out of the country. During his time in the states, he married a woman on his 40ᵗʰ birthday just because he wanted to be married. He later discovered she was not his soul-mate. That marriage only lasted a year. His relationship with her two teenage children was not good because of their continual disrespect of their Mother. He had not been raised like this so this led to many issues in their relationship. He returned overseas as soon as he could deciding that the United States did not satisfy the lifestyle he had become accustomed to. He was a well-known entertainer and enjoyed this life in the limelight. He relates that one night while performing, he was approached by a beautiful woman who later become the Mother of his daughter. Subsequently, he fathered a child but had little involvement in her life. When he returned overseas, he reunited with another old girlfriend and they were married a few years later. This woman had a son the same age as his daughter. She had proven to be very supportive of him while he was still trying to discover himself and further his entertainment career. He was a bit "free-spirited" and needed the support of someone who was grounded. She loved him and was there for him every step of the way. They are now enjoying a good life together in Germany and he is now a responsible employee with a German company. Although he still pursues his entertainment, he has learned that he needs more stability in order to provide for a family. He has reached out to his daughter and was invited to attend her wedding. They are now working on resolving their relationship issues and getting to know each other.

My third son is quite intelligent, handsome and has a great business mind. He was destined to be born and God has a definite plan for his life. He was always the book worm, taking after his Mother in his quest for knowledge. We would sit together and read a lot of times while his older brothers were outside playing. He actually got books and learned how to play certain sports stating he wanted to know how to play by the book so they would not hurt him while "rough housing." His knowledge earned him the recognition of "All Europe" in sports during his senior year in High School while we were stationed in Germany. He joined the Air Force and got a plush assignment right out of school. He was a likeable guy and was very smart. He met his wife while serving in that plush assignment. He always liked children and wanted to have enough for a team! However, they were not able to conceive and later adopted a baby girl. His father-in-law was a small business contractor and he had taught his daughter all he knew. My son, on the other hand, did not have the skills to handle tools, but he had business sense. They combined their skills and started a home improvement business that God continues to bless. They even gave my middle son a job during the time he was making his way back to Europe. They have a great relationship, a beautiful and smart daughter and have been married 25 years.

Every family has their dysfunction and we had ours. I tell people that dysfunction started in the Garden of Eden with Adam and Eve as a result of their disobedience. They may have thought their sin in eating a piece of forbidden fruit was not that bad, but it impacted their sons and every generation afterwards. When Adam and Eve sinned, their sin was against God, but when Cain killed his brother Abel their sin was against their parents and God. This should be a lesson for all of us. Sin may start out as a small thing but it will grow to have a major, long-lasting impact on the entire family.

Our family's "curse" of sexual immorality has touched almost every one of our lives. My knowledge is it began with my maternal grandfather, whom I never met. My Mom told me the story of her father having another family that lived up the hill from where she and my Grand-mother lived. My Grand-mother would help take care of his other children while providing for my Mom, their only child. During those days I guess it was something you just didn't question, you just accepted it. This spirit has impacted my family and some of our family members struggle with sexual immorality that has led to their having children out of wedlock and different sexual orientations.

Because we were such a close family, we were always around each other and some of my family members are now reporting having been touched when they were kids inappropriately by other family members. This has become unspoken behavior in many families. Factors such as no one believing that it really happened, individuals not wanting others to think they were at fault for what happened or not wanting to ruin the family relationship or start trouble within the family have contributed to this "secret." But by burying these behaviors, the root of sexual immorality has not been addressed and has had a detrimental impact on many of our lives. My prayer is that families will see this as a behavior disorder and address it before it ruins families.

There were often times I wanted the family to sit down at one of our many family gatherings and confront these behaviors, but I too did not want to bring them up because of the pain they would cause. But now it's time to deal with these behaviors so we can stop them and give the future generations freedom from falling prey to these types of demon spirits. What's done in the family is not always good to be kept hidden in the family. We must deal with these behaviors if our families are going to heal. Healing past hurts doesn't mean that they will hurt any less, but it does mean that hurt will no longer control your life. As some of my family members read this book, I know they will feel some kinda way, but they know the truth and the truth will set us all free. I want us to be free. I want my bloodline to be free of plaque and those other diseases that prevent free blood flow. Everyone in my family knows God, my Mother made sure of that. The blood of Jesus covers each and every one of us and I thank God for his forgiveness. We can live through these things and find joy in this freedom. A healthy future belongs to each of us.

I am very proud of each of my sons and how God has blessed each of their lives. My family didn't always do what was right, but God has kept all of us and we are a blessed family. Although I was young and "dumb" when I gave birth, God had a plan for my sons' lives as well as my siblings and nieces and nephews and he is fulfilling it each day. I am thankful that he gave me my sons. I have often repented for not bringing them up better, but I could only do what I knew to do. Not making excuses, just stating fact. Their struggles have helped to make them into the mighty Men of God they are today. I pray every day their lives will be remarkable and they will come face to face with their demons and grow pass any residue our family issues may have caused. God has a plan for each of them which began when I asked God to give me boys instead of girls. Who knew how it would turn out!!

LIVING OR JUST SURVIVING

Sitting and glancing ever so pensively out of my home study window, God's glory enlivens me! The colors have changed from the vibrant green that surrounded the lakeside and now reveal a brilliance only God can manifest. We serve a wonderful God. Only He can provide these life watering touches of Himself, just for us, to allow us to experience Him, His power and His presence.

There comes a time in one's life when "enough becomes enough" for many times and situations, but it does not always happen at the same time. What do you mean? Well, just the other day I was wondering how God was going to meet a need that I had. Now, remember, I am a Holy Ghost filled, fire baptized, growing in spiritual maturity, and a woman of God. Wondering, even for a day, or just tying to put a plan in place that you already know mirrors previous efforts, can take you away from the true plan of God. We hear it said to do something different to get something different. However, doing something different to get something different only works if it is ordained by God.

Existing looks the same regardless of the way you look at it. A life inspired by the love of God, the will of God and the manifestation of God, is typically a life of excitement and joy. To simply exist is like going through the motions. You know it's like going around that same mountain, over and over and over and over and over! I think you get the message. But some of us are caught in that cyclical motion and have gotten dizzy. We go around that same mountain, stay in that job, stay in that relationship, continue to buy things we cannot afford, and use food for comfort. All personal choices! Turning to food for comfort because of an injury to our "spirit" at an early age often fuels a life of existing. However, when we use life's circumstances to be a blessing to others, it brings God glory. God never wastes anything. Be it good or bad, God can use it for his glory. Ask yourself, are you living or existing?

Many have written about purpose driven lives over the past 10 years. It all comes back to, bringing glory to God for our life. Some say your purpose began before you were a twinkle in your Mother and father's eyes. Actually, this is quote from the Book of Jeremiah Chapter 1 Verse 5. Even though you may have been born prematurely, out of wed lock, from an adulterous affair, a brutal rape or from young love, God does not see your life as an accident. Whew, that ought to make some of you feel a since of relief as this weight has been lifted from your shoulders. You can truthfully say I am free from the guilt of that mistake that led to my birth or the birth of my child.

We wear the guilt of a situation gone wrong for many years causing us lasting scars. Come on, admit it now. Haven't you had one of those relationships where you thought this person really had your back, only to discover that they had ulterior motives? How often do we surround ourselves with people who do not want to admit their shortcomings but are quick to point out yours? What about those who love to be meticulous about their projects and environments yet lack structure in their personal lives. Once you know a little about people's temperaments, you will be better able to understand what motivates people to behave the way they do. Now, this is not to say that everyone will behave the way depicted by a particular temperament inventory. Environmental and genetic influences are naturally a part of any equation regarding personality temperaments. But these temperament inventories will give you a fairly clear idea about why someone responds a certain way to certain situations.

Life's situations will often not abort the purpose for which God created you. When you wake up every morning with new mercies and undying favor from God, know that your life's purpose has not been fulfilled. We are experiencing a viral pandemic throughout the word at this time. Many people all over the world have died. I cannot say whether they fulfilled their God-given purpose or not. I will say however, that God is the giver of life and calls us to eternal rest. I believe to be absent in the body is to be present with the Lord. My prayer is that you find comfort in believing that their purpose was fulfilled before God called them home.

When the pressures of life seem to be beating you down for the "umpteenth" time, know, with a blessed assurance, that your purpose has not yet been fulfilled so, this too shall pass. These beat downs come to develop your character. Life is a test and every test comes to help us trust God more. Without life's tests, we would never grow. Trials and tribulations are part of life and God will give us the strength to endure. Sometimes when I'm doing home-going services I wonder, God why am I still here? I feel I would willingly exchange places with that person because of all the things going on in the world. However, I know this is selfish and immature. I know God has prepared a place for me in heaven and will determine when my service is done. Consequently, I will still work and give God glory until he calls me home.

What are some of the pressures of life? Money, love relationships, family situations, careers, children. Sometimes pressure comes from being out of the will of God. Yes, that is right, just doing you. When we choose to do us without any regard to the direction available to us from the Holy Spirit of God, we fail to glorify God and thus, reap our own seeds. Yes, these are seeds of disobedience.

These seeds may not result in positive change. Metabolism is what process of changing food into energy. The more we eat, the more active our metabolism becomes which leads to our level of energy. I have been diagnosed with an autoimmune condition call "hypothyroidism" or graves disease which contributes to a slowed down metabolism. This slowed down metabolism contributes to my excess weight making it more difficult to lose weight. There are a large number of people in America who are obese; consequently, there are many products on the market that promise to help you shed those unwanted pounds. Using these get fat off methods only seem to be temporary when they are not accompanied by a life-style change. You may lose the weight over a period of time, but gain back that weight and more soon after you go back to your old habits. These behaviors continue to result in the same outcomes - obesity. This is true of any situation in our lives that is out of control.

Counting the cost of making a lasting health change and deciding that the pain of staying the same, greatly outweighs the pain of change, will help us decide if we want to live or exist. I find that lasting change only comes from life-style changes and being true to oneself about real change. Once we decided to make that life-style change, we start on a journey to live and not simply exist. These choices may be influenced by your family environment.

Take a peek at your family. Certain things you see may give you a glimpse into your future. How long do members of your family live? What led to their death? What lifestyles did they live? How do these lifestyles relate to your choices? Do not be afraid to take this honest look. Family togetherness is important. Our families are by chance, not by our choice. A choice I believe that is made by God. Each person in the family may look or act differently, yet if you look closer, you may recognize some of the same behaviors and beliefs.

I continually seek God to know the plans he has for my family. Until a few years ago, we had five generations living that reflected life over several decades. We now have four generations going back to the late forties and up to the twenty-first century since my Mom and Dad passed over the past five years. What journey does God have in store for this Bloodline? Are we living or are we just existing? We have been gathering over the past approximately 10 years every other year for our five-day family reunion. Most of the family participates, even our first-cousins and extended family friends. The reunions have typically been planned by the second-generation siblings, but as the younger generations begin to plan our events, they are stretching us and taking us outside our comfort zones. They are choosing places further away from our home states and focusing more on including topics for discussion that relate to leaving a legacy and discussions of how we are living, not just existing. I look forward to this generation helping to shape our future lives so that we will have a lasting impact on the upcoming generations. These types of changes in our families will help us define what it means to live and not just exist. I look forward to seeing these positive lifestyle changes taking place within our Bloodline as they begin to introduce these environmental changes.

The environment has a major impact on how we behave. We exist in the space we are in and are influenced by the external forces that surround us. If you find yourself continually and consistently around people who behave a certain way, or who have a certain personality, one day you may look at yourself and see that your "space" partner's behavior has had an impact on you. Whoever has the dominant personality, will normally be the one with the twin in the space. Be careful of who you choose to put in your space. Their choices may soon become your choices and define whether you are living or existing.

Take the challenge and determine how your life is progressing. Ask yourself, "Am I living or existing?" One way that may help you determine your purpose in life is looking at your SHAPE! Yes, physical shape is important but this is a different shape. SHAPE is an acronym that reflects your Spiritual gift, Heart or Passion, Ability, Personality and Experience. It was coined by Rick Warren and can be found in his original book Purpose Driven Life, published in 2002. I encourage you to set aside some serious time and determine the answers to these factors. Determining your SHAPE will help you learn to live your life on purpose and not merely exist.

There will be many distractions, hindrances, or "rabbits to chase" on the way to purpose, put do not give in, the end has already been prepared for you. You just have to continue to travel the journey. Either you do or you do not, either you will, or you will not. Choose ye this day! It really is up to you. Decide whether living or existing best suits your case. And remember your life belongs to God. He is the Creator and we are his masterpieces. Everything we are reflects who God has allowed us to be on our way to achieving our purpose. God created us for this time, this purpose and this place in all areas, physically, spiritually, and mentally. Live by and believe the Scripture that tells us that Jesus came that we might have life and have it more abundantly. Living or existing is your choice. You are a gift to somebody and it is reflected in your past, current and future. Live, don't just exist!

CANNOT GIVE UP OR GIVE IN

I have found much strength in the Word of God. One of the key Scriptures I meditate on day and night is "I can do all things through Christ who gives me the strength." The key is "through Christ." The word "can't" used to be very much a part of my vocabulary. I allowed the stress of dealing with difficult people or having supervisors who were not as forthcoming in their supervisory responsibilities make me want to quit my job. But just as soon as those thoughts came to mind, I chose to change my mind. I would remind myself that I had made it before and I will make it this time. When I discovered that my supervisors did not always have a grasp of the myriad of tasks that I was performing, I would never let a performance evaluation period go by without providing input. Sometimes, writing the entire evaluation myself. My submissions were generally accepted certifying that I was performing these duties which led to higher level qualifications. This further equipped me for higher grade level positions. Remember, just because it is not your job, if you can do it and your supervisor allows it, then take on those extra duties and later you will experience the benefit.

My work life was expressed by excellent performance. The times that I really wanted to run away were those times when I felt people just didn't seem to get it. I was always teaching and continually giving instructions on how an assignment or project should be performed. Oftentimes the people would sluff off the instructions, not pay attention to details, or take short cuts. I later came to understand that some of them just did not get it, did not have the skills to perform the assignment or just did not care. But I would not tolerate inefficiency, lack of responsibility, or sloppy work. I valued excellence. When I became the supervisor, I found myself counseling employees to help them improve and frequently clarifying their job duties. Sometimes there was conflict, but in the end the employee appreciated my instructions commended me for my honesty and willingness to push them to become better. These opportunities always resulted in a better end product. I do not consider myself a confrontational person, so whenever that was a lot of contention, I would just change jobs. I chose not to be in an unhealthy work environment and often took the high road that led to other opportunities. I have since learned to trust God more which has helped me understand that some situations require me to stand and be the change that I wanted to see. Not giving up or giving in requires trust in God.

THE CHOICE IS YOURS

I took a three-month sabbatical from the church where I pastor at the beginning of the year that the viral pandemic broke out. I vowed to organize my study and finish writing this book. While organizing my home study, I ran across a typed sheet of paper that caught my attention. Not that I did not run across lots of other papers since I was "shredding my life" from the 1970s to present. This paper was titled the "Commandments for My Life". These commandments were mostly focused on relationship building. I remember following these commandments diligently for a few years back in the seventies and then somewhere I got lost. There were 13 of these "commandments." Please allow me to highlight a few of them with the application in this work.

Do not Make Promises you may not be able to keep. That will discourage my trust in you.

People will often, without forethought, commit or promise to do something that somehow does not always work out. I know we have all made promises and sometime something may have come up that affected our being able to carry out the promise. Think about a time when you made a promise and the finances required to bring about that promise did not materialize. Or maybe a time when you promised to be somewhere and something came up that required more of your attention and you changed your direction. When things continue to affect your being able to stick to commitments, check your value system. What really is important to you? My Mother always told me to be able to take care of myself and not rely on a man or anyone else to take care of me. That wisdom has been the foundation for most of my decisions. It was what caused many of my sisters and me to obtain employment outside the home. My Mother was a homemaker. Raising eight children and taking care of a husband was her career and she wanted more for us. She never went past the eighth grade in school, but she was a smart, thrifty minded, creative and giving servant. She had what was called "Mother-wit." She impressed upon us girls to get out there and learn how to take care of ourselves. I remember hearing her say "any woman should not have a problem getting anything she wants." I have never been the type to really ask any one for anything. I was and am too independent, whatever that is! I worked to earn the money necessary to buy what I needed. I promised to always hold myself accountable, before making someone else responsible for me.

Another commandment was . . .

DO NOT SPOIL ME. I KNOW QUITE WELL THAT I OUGHT NOT HAVE ALL I ASK FOR. I AM JUST TESTING YOU.

Having an independent nature was one of the issues in my marriage. I started working when my youngest son was about one. Rarely would I ask for anything unless I was something I really needed at the time. Sometimes I would ask to see if the person was really going to give it to me. I saw "quid pro quo" so many times people giving other people things and wanting something in return. That was my red flag. Especially if I was not willing to barter!!

Being independent was a blessing and a curse. Dealing with men who were insecure or intimidated by my independence made it difficult for me to remain in a committed relationship. I used "quid pro quo" when the person had something I wanted. This was BC (Before Christ). I had several friends who valued my independent nature. One of them would send me small care packages filled with little things he thought I could use, just because. These packages included stuffed animals, a model of my dream car, a mini vacuum for my computer, which actually proved to be very handy, and lots of gemstones. He loved stones, which was reflective of his Native American heritage and on occasion he would send me a piece of jewelry with the amethyst stone or brown gemstone. He was a former Marine who had experienced a life filled with transitions. He had even been homeless at some point and was separated from his family for many years. He was thoughtful and caring and promised to give me my dream car, a blue 450SL Mercedes Benz me when he "made it" in life. As I write this book, I am sorry to share that my special friend passed away. He was a loner and didn't socialize with many people. As he lived, so he died. He was found dead from natural causes alone in his apartment. He had been there a week before anyone discovered him. We had talked about three weeks earlier and all was well. My heart cries out to him and so many others like him. Please periodically reach out to your family members and friends. Don't let anyone dear to you leave this earth without your having reached out to see about them periodically. Friendships require that you reach out if only through social media. Check on each other.

I was fortunate to have a friend who would periodically tell me to go to the airport to get the ticket he had left waiting to whisk me off to places I had not visited. He was my best friend and always encouraged me to go after whatever I set my sights on. He was one of the only men I had met that did not seem to want something in return. He was self-confident and not intimated by my success. There was 10 years difference in our ages and he just wanted me to pursue my dreams. We had lots of fun together and found joy in driving to various locations to explore the local attractions. Mostly though, it was just to go for the ride. He gave me nice gifts that I probably would never have purchased for myself. One of the first gifts he gave me was a gold cigarette case and lighter. That was during my cigarette and marijuana smoking days. I would roll my joints and put them in the cigarette case along with my Benson Hedges Menthol Light Cigarettes. He later gave me a gold watch and a specially designed pinky ring with a little diamond situated atop an arrow. When we first met, he was in the Air Force but later retired. We remained friends for a long time, but things began to change once we became intimate. We drifted apart and he got remarried and I reunited with my husband. We rekindled our friendship about 10 years later after I returned from Germany. Once I moved back to Virginia, we had an occasional lunch or we just watched a movie at his house. He is an avid movie watcher. He has also supported events at my church and we remain friends today.

My independence became a curse during the time I was married. I was continually reminded that I did not need anyone and that I was too independent. His comments offended me at first, but later as I became honest with myself, I realized he was right. I had lived a life without him for many years and had made a good life for me and the boys. We were separated on and off for the first twenty years of our twenty-five-year marriage. While we were separated, I never pressured him to take care of the boys financially because I was working and did not want him to feel we needed his money or that I was forcing him to do something against his will. If he wanted to contribute toward their upkeep, so be it. But the majority of the time, I took care of our financial needs. My independence may have been a curse for him, but it became a plus for me and helped me to be responsible for the care of myself and three growing young boys.

Some other commandments were:

> *DO NOT LET MY BAD HABITS GET A LOT OF YOUR ATTENTION.*
> *IT ONLY ENCOURAGES ME TO CONTINUE THEM.*

> *DO NOT CORRECT ME IN FRONT OF PEOPLE. I WILL TAKE MUCH*
> *MORE NOTICE IF YOU TALK QUIETLY WITH ME IN PRIVATE.*

> *DO NOT TRY TO PREACH TO ME. YOU WOULD BE*
> *SURPRISED HOW WELL I KNOW WHAT IS RIGHT.*

Many of these commandments deal with attitude. Attitude has always been very important to me. Mine has not always been so positive. Growing up feeling I was constantly overlooked, just made me feel some kinda way. But as I grew in God and in the things of God, I realized the importance of "your attitude determines your altitude." Being true to self helps us deal with that person in the mirror. The Word reminds us that we can look at ourselves then walk away and forget what we look like. We are quick to judge someone else, but forget we have issues too. Whether you have any commandments in life or "life's saying," don't forget to start with the person in the mirror. Examine your heart and remember out of the heart the mouth speaks. The choice is yours!

GOD GETS THE GLORY

I consider choice to be absolute. Synonyms for absolute are total, complete, conclusive, and out-and-out. There are not many things in life that are absolute. Once you make a choice, you have made a decision to do or not to do something. I believe the Word of God is absolute. I believe my relationship with Jesus Christ as the Son of God is absolute. Choice relates to the free-will that God gave all of us to exercise. God is Sovereign and there is nothing that happens that he does not allow, but He will not force us to make any decision. This free-will he gave us allows us to make our own choices. The problem is we often forget that leaving God out of our decisions often ends up leading to uncomfortable consequences. Of course, we want to ask God to remove these consequences, but he has no obligation to do so since we did not seek His will and follow Him in making our decisions. I remember telling my sons, if you don't make me part of the choice, then don't make me part of the consequence. BUT because God loves us so much, he will help us get through this consequence and the next one and the next one. He is always there with us and this promise is true. Regardless of what we choose to do, God says he will never leave nor forsaken us. Remember your choice will always lead to a consequence. Follow God's will and it will be God's consequence.

Some of the choices I made had underlying motives. I did not always seek God first in all that I did. For many years I "made it happen." My Choleric personality temperament, independence and lots of faith, were the foundation for my decisions. Once I put my mind to do it, it was a wrap. Relocating, working, choosing housing, changing jobs, these were some of the instances when I dove forward without checking with God, but was motivated by my own reasons. Let me tell you, God is so faithful! Many of these situations were less than ideal, but God always brought me through them.

Looking back over my life, I realize how much God really loves me and you too! There *was*, I am going to say past tense, one major area that I did not seem to have victory in and that was weight. But it is not over yet. I have read God's answer to weight loss and told I could lose weight by eating what is outlined in the Bible. Scriptures are there to help us yet for some reason my resolve to lose weight has not been realized. It is a mind thing. Once I really accept this and make a commitment to change my mind about my eating and exercising, then I will begin to experience the results of weight loss. It must be a life-style change.

Everything else I achieved in life began with a thought. I put the thought at the forefront of my mind and meditated on it daily. I have started many diet programs as many of you probably have also, which only resulted in temporary weight loss. The proverbial key is "It's a lifestyle change." You cannot try it for three to six months, lose a few pounds and then go back to the eating behaviors and lack of movement you had before. The weight comes back and brings more of its sisters' and brothers' pounds with it. It reminds me of a Scripture in the Bible that says when an unclean spirit is cast out of a person it moves around looking for someplace else to occupy. When it does not find a place, it returns to the person bringing with it seven other spirits that are more wicked than him. My mind tells me that my body needs to get moving and I need to feed my insides with foods that are nutritional and better for me at this advanced age. In addition, sitting down too much and not walking or doing simple exercises does not help the cause. I want to be around until my 90s as both my parents were, if it is "God's will" for me to do so and be healthy. I want to have a good quality of life and be able to care for my physical needs should God grace me with those years. I want to have quality time with my great grand-children and see them grow into healthy and mature adults. I encourage you to pray for my focus and commitment.

The motives for many of my choices were rooted in a desire to be better, to learn more, attempt pursuits that would result in increased skills and often increased cash and status, even to prove to someone else that I could do it. My primary reason for returning to high school was so that I could attend college. After starting and completing the first academic degree (Associates), I wanted the next level (Bachelors), then the next level (Masters), then the next level (Doctors). I was driven to achieve higher levels of education. Advanced education has helped me exercise my gifts of teaching and administration. The more I worked in administrative positions in the government, the more confident I became in program administration. Training the workforce in various employment and personal growth subjects was my favorite thing to do. I also learned as I did what I enjoyed. I chose to do what I did not know how to do so that I could learn and grow. This may seem a small thing, but when you have been chosen to teach others, you choose to do your best and at least want to appear that you know more than your students. My choice!!

My motive has always been to leave a place better than it was when I came. This included equipping the people to be better as well. This has been my primary motivation in life. Regardless of how I may have pushed, manipulated, or pissed people off, it was always to get the best out of them. Many times I heard "you have potential." Now I say the same to others. People have so much in them and because of fear or lack of support, they don't try to reach that potential. My life's desire is to encourage the people God put in my path to reach their potential.

This concludes some of the primary facets of my story. There is more to come and I encourage you to prepare to tell your story. You never know who will benefit as a result of your transparency. God purposed that our lives would be great and that we would live in abundance. Whatever that means in your life, reach it. Don't delay. Let this writing prompt you to share. God bless each of you for taking the time to spend with me as I shared my life's journey. May something that was said take root in your heart and cause you to grow.

My motto in life is "if I can help somebody as I travel along this way, my living will not be in vain." It has been my life's choice to be "unstoppable" and I give God all the glory for my life. It has been an honor to complete my first autobiographical publication. Other GEE (Gooch Enhancement Enterprises) publications include pamphlets on your mind, mouth and a growth plan. I encourage you to pass it on and tell your story. Remember God is no respecter of persons, what He did for me, He will do for you. It is your choice. Choose to be unstoppable!

Printed in the United States
by Baker & Taylor Publisher Services